Becoming Your Own Emotional Support System
Creating a Community of One

T0326077

Becoming Your Own Emotional Support System
Creating a Community of One

Linda L. Simmons, PsyD

Routledge
Taylor & Francis Group
New York   London

First published by

Harrington Park Press®, the trade division of The Haworth Press, Inc., 10 Alice Street, Binghamton, NY 13904-1580.

This edition published 2012 by Routledge

Routledge
Taylor & Francis Group
711 Third Avenue
New York, NY 10017

Routledge
Taylor & Francis Group
27 Church Road
Hove, East Sussex BN3 2FA

PUBLISHER'S NOTE
The development, preparation, and publication of this work has been undertaken with great care. However, the Publisher, employees, editors, and agents of The Haworth Press are not responsible for any errors contained herein or for consequences that may ensue from use of materials or information contained in this work. The Haworth Press is committed to the dissemination of ideas and information according to the highest standards of intellectual freedom and the free exchange of ideas. Statements made and opinions expressed in this publication do not necessarily reflect the views of the Publisher, Directors, management, or staff of The Haworth Press, Inc., or an endorsement by them.

Identities and circumstances of individuals discussed in this book have been changed to protect confidentiality.

Scripture taken from the HOLY BIBLE, NEW INTERNATIONAL VERSION. NIV, Copyright 1973, 1978, 1984 by International Bible Society. Used by permission of Zondervan Publishing House. All rights reserved.

Cover design by Jennifer M. Gaska.

Library of Congress Cataloging-in-Publication Data

Simmons, Linda L.
    Becoming your own emotional support system : creating a community of one / Linda L. Simmons.
       p. cm.
    Includes index.
    ISBN: 978-0-7890-3221-8 (hard : alk. paper)
    ISBN: 978-0-7890-3222-5 (soft : alk. paper)
    1. Self-help techniques. 2. Self-management (Psychology) I. Title.
    BF632.S525 2007
    158—dc22
                                        2007000543

Dedicated to my husband, Chuck,
who has so unselfishly devoted himself
to supporting me in my work.

ABOUT THE AUTHOR

Linda L. Simmons, PsyD, is a psychologist at Midwest Christian Counseling Center in Kansas City, Missouri. Her specialty focuses on treating adults with a variety of mental health problems and issues arising from trauma. Licensed in Missouri, Arkansas, and Massachusetts, Dr. Simmons is a member of the American Association of Christian Counselors.

CONTENTS

SECTION II:
BARRIERS TO CREATING A COMMUNITY
OF ONE

SECTION III:
CREATING A COMMUNITY OF ONE

Foreword

There is hope! Many of us face various psychological conditions such as depression, substance abuse, eating disorders, and physical or sexual abuse. Some suffer in silence, while others actively seek all the support they can find. But what can one do when the much-needed support is not readily available? Linda Simmons offers hope to those who are on their own or have little support from others.

Many of the conditions referenced have concomitant psychological treatments. Most of the empirically supported treatments involve medications, behavioral changes, and restructuring of thinking patterns to produce healthy functioning. However, every approach psychologists and psychiatrists use to treat emotional disorders includes the recommendations for psychosocial support. This support is one aspect of what it means to be a part of a community. Truly, participation in community is both healing and protective for all of us. It is this type of community that Simmons describes in this book.

Unfortunately, few of us experience the kind of community that we need in times of crisis. Perhaps it is the effects of various stressors and the toll they place on relationships that erodes community, or perhaps community was never established in the first place. Whatever the reason for the lack of community, it is this community support that is so important in facilitating healing and recovery. But how do you establish community support in times of crisis? How do you develop relationships when it is often those closest to you who have been the purveyors of hurt rather than sources of encouragement?

Simmons describes a path for developing the kind of nurturance needed in times of turmoil. When I first read about "creating a community of one," I thought it was an oxymoron—kind of like "free rent" or "half true." How can one have community without others involved? As Simmons clearly writes, this is a transitional state on the way toward developing healthy, strong, and supportive relationships with others. She empowers those in the midst of turmoil to develop

Becoming Your Own Emotional Support System
Published by The Haworth Press, Inc., 2007. All rights reserved.
doi:10.1300/5828_a

strategies that provide the kind of support needed for full recovery. Rather than remaining a victim from the actions of others or the misfortune of disorder, she describes ways to actively support oneself on the way to receiving the needed support of others.

This book will help people develop necessary resources to overcome the obstacles to recovery when facing common struggles. Dr. Simmons uses her vast experience as a psychologist to address common problems and her approach empowers people to develop their own support systems rather than await the care of others. Her practical suggestions are a welcome recommendation for those who practice in the mental health field, and an accessible resource for those who experience the challenges and struggles common to so many.

Clark D. Campbell, PhD
ABPP/Clinical Professor of Psychology,
George Fox University

Preface

What is a community of one, how do we create it, and why do we even need it? These questions have formed in my mind over the years in my practice of psychotherapy. The questions have developed as I've watched client after client come through my door without a supportive community in their background or adequate resources to help themselves. These clients often come with unbelievably deep hurts and deficits, often feeling alone and abandoned. Although they may have people in their lives whom we might expect to be helpful and supportive, for many excellent reasons these clients feel they cannot freely access that help and support. Parents may be alcoholics, aunts or uncles might have been perpetrators, spouses may have been unfaithful, or children may have become consumed with chasing after their own success. Money can buy all kinds of support, right? Not if it was never there to begin with. Money may have been spent on medical bills, legal costs incurred by divorce, or wasted on addictions.

A community of one is needed when individuals find themselves in situations, often through no fault or choice of their own, where they have few to no support systems and few to no material resources with which to move forward in healthy ways. Sometimes these situations are temporary and sometimes they are chronic. Typically, individuals temporarily in need of creating a community of one will be better able to grasp the concept and more quickly reconnect with a community of many than those with chronic situations. Those who find themselves chronically in need of creating a community of one will struggle and often experience intense loneliness. Even then, a community of one can be created; it is not impossible. The purpose of this book is to suggest and describe ways of doing exactly that.

Loneliness is one of the most common denominators that drives people to the need of a community of one. It is an unfortunate fact of life that loneliness plagues us all at one time or another. Frequent companions of loneliness are fear, uncertainty, and perhaps feelings

Becoming Your Own Emotional Support System
Published by The Haworth Press, Inc., 2007. All rights reserved.
doi:10.1300/5828_b

of helplessness. Loneliness is a completely different state from that of being alone. Being alone can be a self-reflective, rejuvenating experience—a time to regroup and renew enthusiasm for life. However, loneliness is frequently the result of loss. Loss is a stalker who comes in many disguises. Chronic illness may involve a loss of previous levels of physical functioning. Divorce represents the loss of dreams for a loving marriage that will last happily ever after. Unemployment may lead to a loss of self-esteem as well as financial security. Death of a loved one is the loss of a familiar voice, a comforting touch, a secure presence. The disguises seem unlimited and are always unwelcome.

We are social beings, some of us more so than others. It is rare to find someone living happily and contented as a hermit. As social beings, we expend a great deal of energy forming relationships and communities. Most people find deep satisfaction in connecting with other caring, like-minded individuals. These relationships and communities are the greatest weapons against loss and loss's subsequent companion, loneliness. There are many avenues in which we connect with community, such as through our families, places of employment, places of worship, schools, support groups, and social clubs. Most of us have access to these community and relational supports whenever we feel the need.

However, some life experiences are so unexpected, so overwhelming, so frightening, so shameful or embarrassing, or so repugnant to the rest of society, that we are plunged into that unwelcome state of loneliness. This loneliness can lead us down a path of isolation and despair. We wonder how we will survive because the reliable comforts of relationships and community may seem inaccessible, at least for a time. Our own distorted thoughts and perspectives may also betray us in our search for social support, keeping the light of hope hidden. Depression and anxiety may cause us to misperceive the good intentions of others just as ignorance of those maladies may cause rejecting fear in those who could be helpful.

The goal of a successful community of one is to enable a person to confidently gain access to a positive community of many. As painful as it might be, this requires examining the deficits, problems, and weaknesses in our lives with complete honesty. Only when we can face these difficult areas of our lives with honesty and integrity can we learn and grow from them. We may need to grieve loss, resolve conflicts with others, or forgive ourselves before we can come to a place of acceptance and resolution with our past. Otherwise, the past will be a constant interference in our present and future, robbing us of the confidence and peace necessary to satisfactorily and enjoyably interact with a community of many. Creating a community of one may be necessary because there is no one to walk alongside us in this process or there may be inadequate resources to initially access a community of many. However, one of the major parts of creating a community of one is dealing with those issues that we must face alone—the act of looking in the mirror and honestly coming to terms with where we are in life. There are aspects of that which we have to complete alone, even though there might be others willing to help. This work leads us to a place of self-respect and a clear conscience, both of which are necessary ingredients to moving on to a community of many.

All of this being said, there are many wonderful supports available to help us through these difficult circumstances in our lives: self-help books, therapists, support groups, community resources, clergy, and educational retraining courses among others. Nevertheless, there may be a huge gulf between where we are in life and where we can access those supports. *Becoming Your Own Emotional Support System* recognizes that we do not live in an ideal world. It acknowledges that there may be no easy answers for the painful situations in which we might find ourselves. This book is also written with a great deal of compassion, knowing that we all desire peace and contentment in life's journey and knowing that sometimes feels like an impossibility. *Becoming Your Own Emotional Support System* talks about how we can become an emotional support system for ourselves when the realities of life leave us lonely and alone. It discusses how we can equip ourselves to move forward from places of despair to places of limitless opportunity. I hope that for those who take the challenge of creating a community of one, this will be a starting point to finding peace and relational enjoyment in the life ahead.

The stories told in this book reflect lives that could be real people, although they are composites and not the stories of any specific individuals. These stories are limited and only a sampling of all the stories that could require the creation of a community of one. Unfortunately, I have encountered so many life scenarios that fit this category that it was too easy to draw elements of the stories from many individuals. It is my desire that those who are lonely and isolated will find understanding, comfort, and hope. It is also my desire that others will become more aware of the need to include the hurting in a supportive community of many.

Acknowledgments

Like most writers, I find it hard to know where to begin when it comes to acknowledgements. There is a fear of accidentally leaving someone out who was truly significant in the process of writing this book. However, with that in mind, I want to acknowledge the brave and courageous clients whom entrusted me with their stories of pain, perseverance, and very private struggles. The courage it takes to reveal one's most vulnerable areas to someone who is initially a stranger is unbelievable.

My literary agent, Janice Pieroni, Esq., has been a mentor, an encourager, and most of all, a friend. The process of becoming a writer would have been much more perilous without her guidance. Dr. Lorna Hecker, my editor, has an incredible gift for positive encouragement and I always look forward to her comments and suggestions with great anticipation. I cannot say enough about the staff at The Haworth Press, Inc. Through the wonder of electronic collaboration, I have never met the Haworth Press staff in person, yet they are an ever-present supportive team ready and willing to help with whatever I need. The smallest to the largest questions are always answered quickly, respectfully, and thoroughly. Thank you!

Finally, my family keeps me going. Like Joan in Chapter 2, I have dealt with systemic lupus for many years. At times it has been difficult to accomplish all that I want to do. Without the support of my parents, Rollie and Cleta Frazier, my sister and brother-in-law, Douglas and Debra Millett, and my sons, Samuel and Adam, many of my goals such as writing this book, would have had to be discarded. They have served as my community of support. Thank you as well!

Becoming Your Own Emotional Support System
Published by The Haworth Press, Inc., 2007. All rights reserved.
doi:10.1300/5828_c

SECTION I:
THOSE IN NEED OF A COMMUNITY OF ONE—THEIR STORIES

Chapter 1

"One Is the Loneliest Number": When New Identities Are Forced Upon Us

MARYANNE'S STORY OF DIVORCE

Maryanne was young, vivacious, and full of hope when she met and married Tom. Both were in their early twenties and in college when the sparks flew in economics class. Maryanne had signed up for the class to fulfill her social studies requirement for her education degree. Tom had dreams of becoming a "business tycoon." Maryanne had never dated much. She had always been a serious student with career goals in mind. When Tom insisted on walking her home from class every day, she was completely flattered. He was tall, muscular, and very handsome. His determined focus on his own career gave him a sense of maturity that was missing in many guys his age. From Maryanne's perspective, Tom was the man of her dreams. He was the kind of man she thought would never give her a second look.

Although she lacked self-confidence, Maryanne was driven to achieve as a teacher. She loved children and idealistically believed she could make a difference in the world by becoming a loving educator. In high school, boys had teased her for being so smart, but Tom seemed to genuinely appreciate her intellectual abilities. Maryanne soaked up this affirmation like a hungry sponge. This acknowledgment of her abilities had been missing in her family. Within a few months, Tom proposed marriage and Maryanne took only minutes to consider and accept before he might change his mind. She had already openly discussed with him all the important values in her life: her career, having children, and her faith. Tom had seemed to share these values in every respect. Maryanne had secretly feared that she

Becoming Your Own Emotional Support System
Published by The Haworth Press, Inc., 2007. All rights reserved.
doi:10.1300/5828_01

would never meet anyone who would accept and appreciate her, someone who would want to be her life partner, but now she was well on her way to the perfect life.

This excitement lasted for about a day until she began telling friends of her engagement. The shocked silence from each of them before they quickly recovered and unconvincingly tried to be supportive led to Maryanne's first nagging doubts. "You've only known him a few months," they said. "What's the hurry? What do your parents think?" Maryanne realized that she didn't even want to tell her parents. In fact, they didn't even know she had been dating seriously. Before she could shut it out, the thought crept in that a wedding should be a happy occasion to excitedly share with family and friends. Instead of excitedly calling to share the news, Maryanne was dreading it. Her parents had never seemed to trust her judgment about anything and she feared their expected criticisms. The red flag she most wanted to ignore, and did initially, was that Tom didn't seem to want to help her reassure family and friends.

The wedding date was set for three months away. Maryanne met Tom's family for the first time when they traveled to his parents' home for a bridal shower. They seemed a little odd, but nice enough. It bothered her that Tom became more distant emotionally while visiting his family. He expressed no physical affection at all, even though it didn't seem that his parents would have minded. When she asked him about his behavior, he shrugged her off and said not to worry about it. This especially bothered her because Tom had begun pressuring her sexually as soon as they were engaged. Maryanne's values were such that she wanted to wait for sex until they were married, but Tom convinced her that engagement was practically the same as being married and she had given in. Nevertheless, Maryanne was plagued with guilt. The worst part of their sexual relationship was Tom's anger when she wanted to discuss it.

About two months before the wedding, Maryanne's period was late and she feared she was pregnant. She felt that even though a pregnancy had not been planned or even talked about at this point, Tom would be shocked, then overjoyed and take it in stride. Her idealism regarding Tom completely disintegrated when she realized that he would likely leave her and call off the wedding if she was pregnant. He never said this in words, but every other method of communication shouted it out as being the truth. His silence, stiff posture, and turning away were all messages communicating his true feelings. Maryanne knew she was at a crossroads in the relationship. She could feel the hurtful rejection by her family if she were unmarried and pregnant, especially since they didn't approve of Tom in the first place. Maryanne had been working so hard to convince them that they should trust her judgment in this matter, but now in her heart, she had to admit their judgment was probably correct.

A few weeks later she was greatly relieved to discover she was not pregnant. Tom said nothing. It was as if the crisis had never happened. A combination of shame, guilt, and false pride led Maryanne to bury all her doubts and continue toward the wedding altar. During the ceremony, people were crying, but Maryanne knew they weren't tears of joy. It was not the happiest of occasions, but everyone tried their best to pretend otherwise. The honeymoon was a disaster and there was no question that she had made the biggest mistake of her life. This realization washed over her with sobs that wouldn't stop coming. It was the first time she recognized the depth of Tom's anger, or at least the first time she was forced to face it. If she were honest, she would have acknowledged the subtle signs from early on in the relationship; the hole in the wall of their wedding suite left her no doubt and she recognized his duplicity. Tom lied about his activities in his free time and Maryanne lied to cover everything up. She couldn't bear to have her humiliation made public. Tom seemed not to care one way or the other around Maryanne, but knew his future as a "business tycoon" depended on a respectable home front.

Maryanne got pregnant within a few years of their marriage, a boy first and then a girl two years later. She was certain the children would help her deal with her loneliness. Maryanne loved them dearly, especially since she received no love from Tom. Even though she never returned to finish her college education, Maryanne felt it was a good trade-off and lavished her love of teaching on her two bright children. She supported Tom in every way to help him complete his business degree. It paid off for him. Maryanne knew how to entertain and potential clients were rightfully impressed with her skills. Tom obtained more than a few clients due to her hospitality and creative presentations in the home. After the last guests left, Maryanne often heard how lucky she was that he still stayed with her since she was so stupid and inept. Within a few years, Maryanne believed it, giving up her dream of teaching even after her own two children were in school and she had time and resources to finish her degree.

With each promotion Tom received the family moved to new locations across the country. This meant that Maryanne and the children were never allowed to establish long-term friendships. There was never anyone Maryanne knew well enough to share how awful her life situation had become. Always starting over seemed to be her mantra. Tom, though, met people he knew in each location since he stayed with the same company. Tom's success built him up and, at least in his mind, gave him permission to continue tearing Maryanne down. With no close friends or family around for support, Maryanne turned to food and eventually put on so much weight that she was embarrassed to walk out the front door. It became yet one more barrier that kept her from getting the help she desperately needed. Depression soon followed the weight gain and Tom's constant put-downs kept Maryanne in a pit. She crawled out long enough to care for her children; other than that, the dark pit was her only safe place.

Tom, on the other hand, was moving onward and upward. Not only was his self-confidence growing with each promotion, but so was his arrogance and self-centeredness. It was almost inevitable that he began pursuing other women to share his upward mobility. Maryanne was somewhat aware of what was happening but chose not to believe it. She tried to bring it up a few times and talk about the need to work on their marriage, but for Tom, it was another opportunity to tell her she was crazy as well as stupid. She was so afraid of his anger when she brought up these unpleasant topics that it took everything in her to get all the words out. The holes punched in the walls were coming ever closer to her face. Eventually the fear paralyzed her and she gave up trying.

Then came the day when Tom announced he didn't need her anymore and had found someone more suitable to his successful position. He filed for divorce and custody of their two children. Tom had neglected the children as much as he had neglected Maryanne and she wondered if the sudden desire to be a father was related to his not wanting to pay child support. Maryanne was both devastated and panicked. She had convinced herself that she loved Tom and that in spite of everything, they would be together forever. She was panicked at the thought of caring for herself and her children without Tom. She was in a strange city with no close friends and no family. Even if she had friends and family, she did not feel she could approach them with her situation. Maryanne had told so many lies over the years that many thought she had the perfect marriage; she had wanted that for the sake of her children.

Unfortunately, Tom now had a spotless reputation in public and used it to his advantage. He told people how low Maryanne had sunk into depression. He had said that the children needed to be away from her negative influence for their own good. According to Tom, Maryanne could not even responsibly care for them. Tom manipulated people into thinking that Maryanne was so sick that she might attempt suicide, and the children might find her wounded or dying. As a model father, he could not let that happen, could he? He would never be able to forgive himself! Besides all that, he had a right to his own happiness. In Tom's mind, he had been a martyr long enough, putting up with Maryanne's mental illness and low-class appearance. Donna just happened to come into the picture at the right time. Providential, of course. Tom's lies continued and Maryanne's low self-esteem made it almost impossible for her to fight back.

She never completed her education nor had she worked in years. She had no idea how to begin a job search and with no marketable skills knew that minimum wage would likely be the best she could find. Maryanne was dreadfully afraid of the condemnation she expected from family and friends. Although her depression wasn't as dire as Tom described, it was still serious enough that it made normal functioning impossible. The only thought that kept Maryanne moving forward was that she had to fight for her children. Divorce was forcing Maryanne into a new role and identity that she was completely unprepared to take on. It was a role that, frankly speaking, she had criticized in others. Maryanne had idealistically believed that the only reason people got divorced was because they were too selfish to work out their problems. Any problem could be solved with diligence and hard work, right? Because of her depression, feelings of loneliness, helplessness, and hopelessness were Maryanne's only companions.

MARYANNE'S NEED FOR A COMMUNITY OF ONE

Clearly, Maryanne found herself in a situation where she felt isolated, alone, without emotional resources, and in need of a community of one. How did she get there? Many factors led to Maryanne's need to create a community of one. She had low self-esteem and personal doubts before her marriage. She was naive and didn't recognize emotional abuse or realize how it could affect her. Her husband kept her emotionally isolated so she didn't have close relationships to help her examine her life experiences. Somewhere along the way, Maryanne lost the ability to distinguish the truth about herself from the lies Tom told to maintain his control over her.

Tom's financial control was just as gripping and Maryanne had very few material resources to provide for herself and her children. Emotionally and physically, she would have found it very difficult to hold down a job at this time, in spite of the necessity. Even if others had provided affirmation and encouragement, Maryanne would have found it very difficult to believe them over Tom. She became self-critical about her weight gain and her failure to complete her educational goals. When Tom chose another woman who would be "more worthy" of him, Maryanne believed her own worthiness was gone.

A NEW IDENTITY ENFORCED BY DIVORCE

We hear so much about the high rate of divorce in this country that it seems as if divorce were commonplace. Yet each divorce involves individuals; few people go into marriage even imagining that divorce could be a possible outcome. In spite of the very high divorce rate, most people believe marriage to be a permanent commitment until death. The feelings generated by divorce are varied and unpredictable. Grief, sadness, anger, despair, fear, anticipation, and relief may all be present, depending on the circumstances of the divorce and the time of day. It is a tumultuous time of newness and uncertainty. The individuals involved may not know what to expect on a daily basis and those on the periphery may also have no idea what to expect or how they should react.

For these reasons, divorce not only forces a new identity upon us, but it may also leave us in one of the loneliest places of our lives. Friends and family will most likely want to be supportive but may not know how. If they've had attachments to both partners, they may withdraw out of a desire not to hurt either party's feelings. They may feel confused about taking sides, feeling a need to be supportive of one side and then feeling disloyal to the other. Friends and family

may feel hurt if they were left out of the problems, making the ultimate decision of divorce seemingly delivered out of the blue. Most
likely friends and family will have had other experiences with divorce, possibly their own or that of others they know, which will
influence their reactions as well.

People outside of the broken couple deal with their own responses,
feelings, and reactions to the situation. They may feel anger over the
disruption of the extended family. Whom do we invite to Thanks-
giving dinner? The custodial parent as well as extended family may
be anxious regarding children visiting with a parent who is no longer
trustworthy. Both friends and family may approach the situation very
cautiously, wanting to help a wounded person but also wanting to
make sure that person doesn't become overly dependent. Some individuals, especially family, may worry whether it will affect them financially. Will the divorcing person need to borrow money? Want to
come live with them? Need help with transportation costs, babysitting costs, attorney's fees, or other expenses? New roles and read-
justments in relationships are initially uncomfortable for everyone.
Some will be more able to cope than others.

For all these reasons and more people may withdraw and withhold
their support from the divorcing couple. The resulting sense of abandonment can be raw and striking. The people you always thought
would offer encouragement are suddenly absent. They may eventually come back into your life, but they may not. It is not easy to find
new friends and supports in times of pain. Divorce often leaves us in
such a vulnerable state of neediness that we may not make the wisest
choices in new relationships, especially romantic ones, for a considerable period of time after the divorce. To the divorcing person needing the comfort of supportive human contact, this feels like the with-
holding of a glass of cold water after traveling for a week in the
desert.

RESPONSES TO DIVORCE THAT LEAD TO CREATING A COMMUNITY OF ONE

A helpful approach to loneliness in these types of desperate and
new situations is twofold. First, a person must learn the skill of being
his or her own best friend. This can be a daunting task since many
people avoid being alone because they do not like the company. Self-

hatred makes being your own best friend less than appealing. In her outstanding book, *The Emotionally Abused Woman* (1990), Beverly Engel stated, "All of us travel through life with only one constant companion, and that is ourself. How sad if your closest companion is someone you don't even know" (p. 181). It takes a great deal of courage to look in the mirror and say to yourself, "You seem like someone I'd like to get to know. Let's hang out together and see what happens."

Second, it is helpful if a community of many can take up the slack and come alongside the hurting person. An external supportive community can communicate to the individual that he or she does have value and that he or she is a worthwhile investment. There certainly are some exceptional communities that provide the necessary nurturance and support for an injured person to regain his or her emotional and psychological health. Bravo! May those communities become an example and the norm. In the absence of that, people must develop the skill of being their *own* best friend, in spite of their lack of trust that it could work out to their advantage. In fact, to someone like Maryanne, this may sound like the wildest idea of the twenty-first century. After years of degrading remarks she had heard from her husband, the thought that she could be a desirable best friend to anyone, let alone herself, gave her a good laugh.

Sometimes the support is there but invisible. Have you ever flown in an airplane traveling through a thick fog bank? You can hardly see the end of the wings outside the window. You can only hope and imagine that the runway lights are operational or the ground crew is waiting alertly to guide the plane through the traffic. Some of these overwhelming circumstances are like that fog bank; they make it impossible to see or imagine that help is at hand. The development of trust in something or someone dependable is essential for survival. That trust has to start with yourself. It may be trust that you are a capable person, that you can mobilize your personal strengths on your own behalf, and/or that you can start over and learn new skills to adapt if necessary.

Invisible supports are those that are present and available but may be unknown to the person in need. The person might know about these supports, but never imagine they could apply to him or her. For example, Maryanne knew about a divorce support group in her community, but had paid little attention to it since she had thought she would never need such a service. She had seen advertisements at the grocery store for the local Parents Without Partners group, but had dismissed them in order to check out the weekly sales. Now that Maryanne was a single parent these potential supports grabbed her attention, but first she had to admit to a new identity. This new identity fit very appropriately in these types of groups. At some point, she might even begin to consider that this new identity could be a positive one.

Maryanne had gone through a three-step process in the course of her life: from low self-esteem to an emotionally abusive marriage to serious depression and feelings of helplessness. Although all three problems are complex and difficult to resolve, the serious depression should be the place to start. In her depressed state, Maryanne was finding it difficult to concentrate, think clearly and rationally, and remember things she needed to do. She had little energy due to her lack of appetite, poor eating habits, and lack of sleep. Her feelings of hopelessness and helplessness led to a lack of motivation to change her circumstances. Physically, Maryanne needed help before she could effectively address the other issues. Luckily, she still had health insurance that enabled her to see her doctor and begin an antidepressant medication. Maryanne also began seeing a therapist.

What about those individuals who don't have the financial resources to get that kind of help? Many states provide some type of health care for those who are uninsured. Doctors may have sample medications or a person might contact a drug company directly to ask for assistance. It certainly doesn't hurt to ask. If a person lives near a counseling or psychology training program, he or she might be able to receive counseling services at minimal or no cost from student counselors or psychologists in training. These students are required to have a licensed professional supervising and directing the treatment, so the treatment is often quite good in spite of the student's lack of experience. Many therapists often take on a few cases pro bono as a means of community service. Again, taking a risk to ask for this type of help may result in much-needed assistance.

A more difficult problem for someone like Maryanne to address is that she chose to marry an emotionally abusive man. According to Mary Susan Miller (1995),

> Emotional abuse takes many different forms en route to the goal of domination, all of which undermine a woman's self-respect and sense of worth. A man may begin with a complaint and slide

into constant criticizing and name-calling before she even senses a problem. He may embarrass her in public by putting her down or screaming. He may accuse her of having lovers and begin watching her every move, stalking her when she meets a friend. He may walk away when she tries to talk to him or pout and not speak to her for days at a time. He may throw accusations and curses at her parents and other relatives with whom she is close. He may forbid her to make decisions or offer an opinion in family matters and even in her own affairs. The emotionally abused woman lives in a state of fear: what will the man do next? (p. 25)

Maryanne could have easily identified with much of this description of an emotionally abusive man. Even though his behavior was not her fault, Maryanne felt stupid for not recognizing the signs, for ignoring her intuition, and for not paying attention to the advice of friends and family. More than anything else, the shame and humiliation that Maryanne felt from making such a poor marital choice isolated her and made it hard for her to believe she was worthy of the companionship of herself or others. Again, Beverly Engel (1990) says it well,

Emotionally abusive lovers and mates can cause tremendous damage to a woman's ego. They have our trust, our vulnerability, our hearts, and our bodies. Using a variety of tactics, an abusive husband or lover can damage a woman's self-esteem, make her doubt her desirability and hate her body, and break her heart. It is incredibly painful to come to the recognition that someone you love and want desperately to believe loves you in return could actually be abusing you. (p. 22)

Although it would have been easier to stay lost in Tom's lies and give up, Maryanne at least knew she wanted to be a healthier person for the sake of her children. Initially that was her sole motivating force to examine what she'd been through.

Once she developed trust in her therapist, Maryanne began to disclose some of the treatment she had received from Tom. She knew that her therapist would keep things confidential unless she were suicidal or homicidal, so Maryanne reasoned that even if the therapist did not believe her, it was only one person and therefore a contained disaster. Maryanne discovered that she was believed, and her therapist encouraged her to connect with other women from similar backgrounds through a support group. There are many places to look for support groups. One can receive recommendations from a therapist or clinic, doctors' office bulletin boards, online Web sites, churches, women's shelters, and so forth. The most difficult part is the first step: dialing the first number or opening one's mouth to emit the first word. Often, the pain of isolation must outweigh the fear of ridicule and rejection before someone will make those first attempts at outreach. This is where the person seeking to build a community of one must call on his or her inner courage, even if he or she does not know if it is there or not.

Once Maryanne was feeling better physically and had a better understanding of Tom's abusive behavior toward her and its effects, she was ready to address the issue of her own self-esteem. This required brutal honesty and was likely the most challenging part of her recovery. Yet healthy self-esteem is one of the foundational pieces in creating a community of one. Maryanne needed to go back to the beginning. She had to ask herself many questions. What were her abilities, talents, and gifts? What were her areas of weakness? (She came up with those easily.) What were the hopes and dreams she had as a child, adolescent, and young adult? Where did they go? She knew she had not fulfilled them.

It was time to find out the answers to these questions. By this time, Maryanne was adamant that she did not want to be defined merely as a "divorced woman." A new identity was in order. This time the new identity needed to be one of her own choosing, not one imposed on her by someone else. Too often we define ourselves by an event or by circumstances and carry that definition throughout our lives. Yet events and circumstances are *not* the soul of who we are. Maryanne instinctively recognized that, even though her feelings did not always match up.

What is healthy self-esteem? It is taking the light of this brutal honesty and shining it into every aspect of our being. It is recognizing and owning our strengths, recognizing and owning our weaknesses, and also recognizing and owning our mediocrity. Healthy self-esteem makes good use of our strengths, works on correcting our weaknesses, and works on improving or accepting our mediocrity. It maintains a standard of excellence in the way we live our lives but also acknowledges that perfection will not be attained in our earthly lifetime. As we recognize and come to terms with all these pieces of our lives, we will attain an overall sense of peace and contentment with our self that results in acceptance.

When a person finds himself or herself in a situation such as Maryanne, where a new identity is forced upon them, there are three options. One can spend time focusing on the past identity, grieving it, longing for it, and believing that its return is the only thing that will make life better. Although it is normal and necessary to grieve our losses, it is counterproductive to stay in that place. Second, one can numb their emotions, blunt their thinking, and try to maintain the status quo. This choice only serves to help a person survive, not to live. Sometimes the circumstances we are faced with are so overwhelming that we "numb out" to survive, but to stay there is to be physically alive and emotionally dead. Third, after the grieving is done, one can choose to develop a new identity.

This last option can be a great adventure, a time to explore unknown territory, and an opportunity to do things differently. This approach is the beginning of creating a community of one. It requires courage, imagination, the willingness to take risks, and the development of a vision or dream of the life you really want. Even if it all feels unreachable at the present time and no path seems clear, there is a belief that a way exists and a determination to live toward the future.

Chapter 2

May I Introduce You?:
Discovering Our Lost Selves

JOAN'S STORY OF CHRONIC ILLNESS

One of the most devastating discoveries we face when forced to play a new role or take on a new identity, is that we are no longer comfortable in our own skin. The question "who am I?" covers territory from our head to our toes and from our skin to our capillaries. We may not know how we work physically, mentally, emotionally, or spiritually anymore. We may not be able to identify our true desires, beliefs, values, or goals. We may not even know how we would like to wear our hair, dress ourselves, or wear our makeup. When we look in the mirror, we see ghosts with no form or substance. These thoughts, feelings, and perceptions may last a few seconds, a few days, a few weeks, or a few years. However long it lasts, discovering the answer to "who am I?" can either be one of the most terrifying journeys we will ever take or one of the most exciting.

Six months ago, Joan returned from her doctor's office in a state of total shock. She had gone to get a physical because she was "tired of being tired." She had also noticed rashes on her arms and legs and wanted to find out if she was allergic to something that caused such redness and itching. In addition, her joints had been achy, she was running a low-grade fever, and her stomach was a bit upset. She wondered if she had a strange kind of flu or if she was just overstressed. With the prodding of her husband, Joan had decided that she needed professional assistance to overcome the problems. Her husband was tired of hearing her complain of all these symptoms. It seemed that every time he suggested they do something fun together, her "little ailments" interfered. Initially, Joan had tried all kinds of over-the-

Becoming Your Own Emotional Support System
Published by The Haworth Press, Inc., 2007. All rights reserved.
doi:10.1300/5828_02

counter remedies with no success. She hated taking time out of her busy days to see a doctor, but she had run out of options.

It had been several years since she had undergone a general physical exam. She was only twenty-seven, so annual physicals when there were no problems had seemed unnecessary to her. Dr. Smith had listened to all her complaints, completed a physical examination, and ordered some blood tests. A week later, Dr. Smith requested that Joan come in for a follow-up appointment to go over the test results. When Dr. Smith walked into the office, she had a grim expression on her face and Joan immediately had a feeling of dread. The doctor shared her findings that Joan had systemic lupus erythematosus or lupus for short. Joan barely heard Dr. Smith's explanation. She had never even heard of this disease and was in a state of shock. Dr. Smith had referred Joan to a rheumatologist whom she highly respected. After more lab tests, the diagnosis was confirmed. Even now, six months later, Joan couldn't quite wrap her mind around what this meant. All she knew was that when she looked at herself in the mirror, she saw a stranger.

This disease of the autoimmune system had so many twists and turns that it was hard for her to understand and almost impossible to explain to family and friends. The one thing she knew was that it was incurable and had changed her life forever. Some of her favorite activities were no longer possible. She had loved to ski and had found challenging courses exhilarating. Not any longer. Her knees were uncooperative, the sunlight hurt her eyes, and her energy level limited her to one run at best. Even her future plans for having children and being an active, involved mom might not be achievable now. It wasn't that she couldn't get pregnant, but it was possible the pregnancy might be complicated. There were many unknown factors. Then too, Joan wondered if it was fair to bring a child into the world with a mother who couldn't fully participate in his or her life. Joan's husband was also reluctant about parenthood now, realizing that he would likely have more responsibilities than he had originally anticipated. This was something to grieve over all on its own, apart from the lupus. Joan felt her body had betrayed her and should belong to someone else. Not only that, but her emotional state often changed seemingly from minute to minute. She felt optimistic and hopeful one minute then depressed and discouraged the next.

The hardest aspect to deal with was the loneliness. Joan didn't know anyone close to her who had such an illness. At first, she was overwhelmed with the concern and offers of help from her friends and family. However, as the weeks and months went on and her condition deteriorated rather than improved, she noticed the calls and e-mails diminished. People stopped asking her to explain the disease so they could understand better what was going on. She noticed that some even had reprimanding tones to their voices, which she interpreted as saying, "why don't you get over it and get on with your life." She didn't know if she was imagining it or not, but Joan felt that people might even think she was dragging it out to enjoy the sympathy and attention. This was silly of course, but Joan felt she couldn't trust her own perceptions.

It was hard to think clearly about anything anymore. Joan had always considered herself a levelheaded woman, but this disease placed all of her old "self and other" perceptions into question. One thing she was sure of—both she and her friends and family were getting tired of having to handle this situation. Except Joan did not have the option of changing the subject. "Who am I and whose body am I in?" Joan asked herself. "Why should I have to take on a new identity when I was quite content with the old one?" Joan was very angry and didn't even know if she had a right to feel that way. Moreover, with whom should she be angry? Herself? God? Her family? Her doctor? She was afraid that if she expressed the extent of her anger, she would be further rejected and made to feel self-centered. The truth was that Joan indeed felt self-centered. She was facing an enemy from within and she didn't know what to do. She knew that her husband was struggling also, but she felt she had nothing to give him.

What Joan didn't realize was that even though her chronic illness may have changed the identity she imagined for herself and the ways she fulfilled her roles in life, it didn't have to change her basic sense of self. Unfortunately, in grieving her changes and losses she lost sight of her core self. Although understandable, it was terribly disconcerting. The grieving process took up incredible amounts of time and energy. The energy, in particular, was in short supply. Joan went through all the typical stages of denial, anger, depression, and bargaining more than once, and couldn't even begin to think about acceptance. Self-doubt and confusion seemed to identify her more than any other descriptive terms.

Joan could not believe that at twenty-seven years old something like this could have shattered her life. It didn't help that most of the time she looked perfectly healthy on the outside. She frequently heard comments from friends and family that she looked great. When her husband made these types of remarks, she never knew if they were meant for encouragement or if they were meant to imply she needed to be getting things done around the house. Likely, they all meant well and at times Joan welcomed these comments as they fed into her own denial. At other times, such comments led her to doubt herself and she wondered if they all thought she was just "faking" her symptoms. She felt like a Jekyll and Hyde person and wondered if others perceived her in that way as well. It took several visits to professionals to help her face the reality that she indeed had a chronic illness that wasn't easily understood and that those around her might also sometimes prefer the avenue of denial.

Then came the bargaining. It primarily took the form of acknowledging that she hadn't always taken the best care of herself. Joan thought she must have brought this on herself because of her poor eating habits, lack of consistent exercise, not taking the appropriate vitamins, and on and on. She bought every book she could find on systemic lupus and studied every type of diet and alternative medicine program on the market. Joan felt that if only she could comply with these various health regimens her symptoms would go away and it would all be a bad dream. However, she found that many of these "cures" were expensive and either hard to find or impossible to adhere to for long. Moreover, it was embarrassing socially to constantly be saying, "I can't have this or that," or "I'm on a special diet and brought my own food," or "I know it looks odd, but standing on my head for ten minutes three times a day really is going to help." People began to wonder if Joan was just very odd and the social invitations steadily declined.

At this point, anger took center stage in a major way. Joan was furious that she had to deal with her problem at all. Although she would never have wished it on anyone else she was still angry that she had been marked. She was angry at the negative impact it was having on her marriage and family life. Her husband's ability to respond in a kind and understanding manner to "I'm so tired" was wearing very thin. She was angry that her time and energy were now taken up with managing an illness rather than doing things she actually enjoyed.

She was angry that relationships with friends were becoming strained. She was angry that her illness was costing a lot of money and at the same time forcing her to work less and less. She was angry that her dreams of having children were in dire jeopardy. Joan was angry because she no longer knew who she was apart from this illness.

After several months, Joan realized that she had to use what fight was left in her to manage her life in a positive manner rather than fight against things that couldn't be changed. The alternative was allowing the disease to destroy her spirit as well as her body. It was the beginning of acceptance and trying to resurrect her core self. Joan spent many hours reflecting, remembering, and rediscovering who she was apart from a body that was less than acceptable at the present. She journaled, re-read books that had been meaningful in the past, studied old photographs, prayed, and meditated as part of her quest for the real Joan. Could it be a new and improved Joan? The jury was out.

Joan recognized that first, she had to thoroughly know her enemy. Dr. Daniel Wallace (1995), in his pivotal book on lupus, stated that lupus

> results from multiple factors. It begins when certain genes predisposing an individual to lupus interact with environmental stimuli. These interactions result in immunologic responses that make autoantibodies (antibodies to one's self) and form immune complexes (antigens combined with antibodies). Certain autoantibodies and immune complexes are capable of causing the tissue damage typically seen in lupus. (p. 33)

Joan discovered quickly why she was often confused about her illness and why it was so difficult to communicate about it to others. To thoroughly understand lupus, as with many chronic diseases, one had to learn a completely new and complicated vocabulary. Unless one had studied the biological sciences in college, the basis for the understanding of disease was illusive at best. It was definitely not material for casual conversations or easy answers to curious questions. No wonder many people lost interest quickly and often regretted asking for explanations.

Joan could readily see that to know her enemy was going to require initiative, time, and dedicated energy. The disease itself kept these resources in short supply. In spite of the difficulties, Joan began small excursions to the local library. The subject of lupus was too complicated to read one book or magazine article for understanding and purchasing the books she needed and wanted was cost prohibitive. She used the library's free internet services as well as the library staff's expertise in research. Through her doctor's office, she heard of short classes offered for patients. Sometimes these classes were sponsored by drug companies, sometimes by various lupus support groups. Joan didn't mind going alone to these groups as she realized that other people there shared with her a common concern. It took weeks and even months before Joan felt she really had a handle on what she was dealing with, but knowing her enemy cut her fears down to more realistic proportions.

JOAN'S NEED FOR A COMMUNITY OF ONE

Joan had already begun to recognize intuitively that she needed to create a community of one for herself. How did she come to this conclusion? After spending a little time with her illness, Joan realized she didn't know or understand herself anymore. Those around her were also confused. Joan needed the support of friends and family desperately, but knew she couldn't communicate her needs adequately if she didn't even understand herself. As the shock wore off, she began to see that all the old answers with which she was familiar no longer fit the questions. Joan had always thought of herself as a young woman enjoying life in a relatively new marriage, poised for a successful career in business, and starting a family. The two children to come were already named and preschools chosen. The house plans that she and her family would occupy were firmly imagined in her head. Joan thought she had already identified her lifelong friends and the church where her two children would be baptized.

Now nothing fit the way she had planned. She felt like she had been working on a thousand piece ocean picture puzzle, had half of it together, and then realized the rest of the pieces must have gotten mixed up with the desert puzzle. Joan was trying to sort the pieces and it was overwhelming. She wanted to complete the ocean picture she had started, but with some of the pieces being so different and maybe some lost it seemed hopeless. She had asked for help from her husband initially, then from others in her circle of family and friends. Through their own observations, Joan's family members and friends recognized her life was not going as expected. However, they were trying to fit together the pieces of their own lives in ways that made sense to them. Joan was therefore compelled to work on her life puzzle alone much of the time. She needed to create a new picture, a community of one.

Although lupus is not a rare disease, it was not something that Joan knew much about. Nor did she know of others in her circle of family and acquaintances who had experience or knowledge about lupus. In addition, lupus can be a chameleon type of illness, mimicking many other ailments and changing symptoms with each flare. Therefore, what Joan had to work with was not always a clear-cut, mapped-out course to follow. Just when she thought she was beginning to get a handle on things and was ready to jump back into her community of many, things changed. This uncertainty about her future made it very difficult to share and communicate with others. This was especially true in her marriage. Joan's husband also had a life puzzle he was putting together and they had both thought their pictures were complementary. Joan's puzzle was an ocean scene and her husband's had been a beach house. If Joan's life puzzle were changing to one of a desert, how would a beach house complement that?

Most of all, Joan needed to create a community of one because of the loneliness her chronic illness had brought her. She felt so different and cut off from all she knew. Joan had never planned on living in a desert puzzle, she loved the water. She knew all the skills required to live around an ocean—she could sail a boat, swim, and knew how to read the tides. She was fascinated by aquatic creatures and was learning how to scuba dive. Joan knew about the most fashionable swimsuits to wear each year and made sure she fit into them nicely. There was language indicative to living around an ocean and Joan and her family and friends knew it well.

Joan knew nothing about living in a desert puzzle. She didn't know the language, the terrain, the clothes to wear, or the skills necessary to survive. Her imagination told her the desert was only filled with prickly cacti, sagebrush, and excessively hot temperatures. There were likely scorpions and lizards under every bush. Joan couldn't imagine anyone choosing to live in a desert puzzle, certainly not her, and maybe not her husband, family, or friends. Joan needed to create a community of one in which her new desert puzzle could display the beautiful blossoms on the cacti, the gorgeous desert sunsets, and the fascinating crystals in the sand. There would be a new language to learn, new friends to make, and she could create an inviting environment in which her old friends and family would enjoy visiting. In order to effectively deal with her loneliness, Joan realized she would have to learn to be alone in her new desert puzzle.

Finally, Joan needed to create a community of one because she was losing many of her old resources. She was discovering she might not have the physical stamina necessary for a demanding career, which could require long hours and frequent travel. This meant that the family income would be cut significantly. Not only that, but her medical costs were rising at an alarming rate just as her income was dropping. Joan felt guilty because at this point much of that burden was falling on her husband. Even though in their wedding vows they had promised to remain together in sickness and in health, for richer or for poorer, Joan was unsure if that would hold true. At the time of their wedding, those kinds of promises had seemed easy to make because they were so unlikely to be needed. This scenario would call on her husband to make sacrifices as well as Joan herself. She had never had occasion to see if her husband had that kind of character and she was afraid to ask or trust.

CHANGES WROUGHT BY CHRONIC ILLNESS

Individuals facing the onset of a chronic illness typically have a steep learning curve to overcome. Irene Pollin (1995) stated that, "The related terms 'chronic illness,' 'long-term medical condition,' and 'disability' encompass an enormous diversity of conditions" (p. 3). She describes categories of chronic illness based on their physical impact:

> Some long-term conditions are degenerative, such as multiple sclerosis (MS), Parkinson's disease, and amyotrophic lateral sclerosis (ALS). Some are protracted and normally lead to either recovery or early death—heart disease and cancer, for example. Some are progressive but normally not life-threatening (arthritis, lupus), while others (such as AIDS and cystic fibrosis) drastically shorten life. According to Pollin, chronic illnesses may be the result of disease, congenital anomalies, developmental conditions, or injuries. (p. 3)

Due to the complicated nature of chronic illnesses, it is easy to see how people can become overwhelmed with a new, unwelcome identity and find themselves in need of a community of one.

How specifically does having a chronic illness lead someone to the place of needing to develop a community of one? The answer may seem somewhat obvious but is actually fraught with many twists and turns; therein is the answer to this question. As with Joan, we often expect certain responses from others and ourselves in certain types of situations, such as being diagnosed with a chronic illness. Sometimes those expectations turn out to be fulfilled exactly as we anticipated. However, we are often caught off guard, taken by surprise, and filled with disappointment not only with the responses of others, but also with our own responses. The very complexity of most chronic illnesses make them difficult to communicate about on a practical level. Friends and family members may not have anticipated the full amount of their time and energy required in helping an ill person.

Others may also feel threatened by the life changes forced upon their ill friend or relative and the realization that life is fragile and finite. Some people are unable to face that fact for various reasons. Simply because the ill person has no choice in the matter of death does not mean they can easily resign themselves to that end and overcome their fears surrounding mortality. Rather, the inevitability of death without being given a choice may strengthen the force of fear. Diseases, such as cancer, that have a long history of painful death have a hard time shaking this reputation in spite of modern medical advances. The very mention of the word cancer, for example, can bring instant fear and hopelessness to the surface. Some people may discover that the very basis of the relationship with the ill person was dependent on that person being a certain way or having certain abilities. When chronic illness removes those personal qualities and abilities the relationship may come up empty and not survive.

Personal goals and dreams may crash into oblivion and never be resurrected in their previous forms. Sometimes our entire life is fixated on working toward a life goal, reaching the highest levels of our careers, or making a stellar contribution in our fields of endeavor. This is often admirable and an individual can attain personal heights about which others only fantasize. However, we can be so focused on a goal and the pursuit of accomplishing it that we become rigid and narrow-minded, able to see little else. Chronic illness can force life flexibility in unimagined ways. If others have merely connected with us to go along for the ride toward momentous goals, they may drop away when those goals must either be given up or drastically altered. "This is not what we signed up for," they say as they shut the door behind them. Chronic illness can certainly determine who our true friends really are.

A person faced with chronic illness may also need a community of one due to a spiritual crisis. He or she may have always believed in God's goodness and love and now feel betrayed. Chronic illness does not present as a loving thing for God to allow. Questions of mortality may arise. Where will I spend eternity? What will eternity be like? Is there an afterlife at all? Am I prepared for death? How do I make peace with God, especially if I'm angry and upset with Him for the predicament I am in? These are common, serious, and legitimate questions that can ultimately only be answered by each individual. Well-meaning, spiritual-minded friends and family may mouth many platitudes in an effort to comfort the ill person, but they may fall very short. In the book of James 1:12 (NIV), it states, "Blessed is the man who perseveres under trial, because when he has stood the test, he will receive the crown of life that God has promised to those who love him." Few people initially feel blessed when receiving a diagnosis of chronic illness and most prefer the crown of life on earth rather than the spiritual crown of life in heaven. This is a struggle whose outcome can only be found in a community of one, no matter how much others might try to help.

There is also the practical impact of chronic illness. Even with health care insurance, a chronic illness can burden the individual and the family with mounting costs. Not only are doctor's visits, medications, tests, hospitalizations, and various treatments very expensive, but there may likely be concurrent deficits in income if the ill person must decrease his or her working hours or resign from a job altogether. Money that was previously available for hobbies and social affairs may now go toward health care necessities. In a household with two incomes, the other spouse may be burdened trying to make up the difference in income. This situation can frequently cause serious rifts or divorce in a relationship, even though the cause of the problem is understood to be the illness and not the "laziness" of the ill person. In some cases, the ill person might be eligible for disability benefits, but actually getting payment started can take many months to accomplish. It can be humiliating to need to make up excuses for friend-related activities due to finances when previously, there was plenty of money. Joan and her husband were struggling with all these issues and it wasn't easy.

Another isolating factor of many chronic illnesses is the change in appearance. Joan struggled with her lupus, which caused ugly rashes and weight gain from medication side effects. Chronic illnesses may be disfiguring or may require the use of awkward appliances such as wheelchairs or walkers. Changes in physical appearance or the addition of mechanical aids can be embarrassing and lead to withdrawal from previously enjoyed social situations. Although many people are understanding about these aspects, the humiliation frequently lies within the patient. This returns to the idea of a new identity, unasked for and unwanted, that has been forced on an individual. Until the patient comes to terms with his or her new and perhaps changing physical appearance, it will be difficult to face others with confidence.

RESPONSES TO CHRONIC ILLNESS THAT LEAD TO CREATING A COMMUNITY OF ONE

After many months Joan discovered the confident awareness that she was a deeply spiritual person who loved people, adventure, beauty, and truth. Although she had her own strong, personal values in many areas, she also appreciated differences in others. She also learned to appreciate the facades people frequently hide behind. In contemplating these things, Joan found a new sense of humility and was ashamed of some of her own previous pretenses. As she became able to forgive herself for her past pride and feelings of superiority, she became more forgiving and understanding of others.

She remembered her enjoyment of the arts and how much she loved being creative. Joan concluded that she had much to offer from the core of her being, although the use of these gifts might be different from her previous assumptions. All of these discoveries and remembrances gave Joan a sense of confidence in who she was apart from her body. Despite admitting that, at times, she might need help from others, she didn't have to be needy. In her new understanding of those around her, their strengths, their flaws, their abilities, and their weaknesses, Joan began to enjoy the mystery of human behavior, including her own. She discovered that chronic illness equalizes all people to the very basics of life.

One of the greatest challenges people face when a new identity is thrust upon them is not only to go through a grieving process, but to then embrace the new identity. This is especially difficult for people with little support in the community or within their families. Sometimes this grieving process puts off potential supporters. It is uncomfortable to be present when someone is experiencing many strong emotions. It may be a reminder of vulnerability which few of us want to face. It takes courage and perseverance to begin a journey of self-discovery such as Joan undertook. However, that in itself can become such a basis of pride and self-confidence that the new identity may come to have more depth and meaning than the old one.

A community of one can become a solid place of refuge for the person suffering from a chronic illness. As peace and newfound confidence in themselves is gained, they can contribute in new and wonderful ways to the community of many. A person can learn peace and contentment by being alone, even with trials and struggles. Having a chronic illness does not necessarily equate with loneliness and isolation. It is not uncommon to initally feel pity when meeting an individual with a handicap, disability, or chronic illness but then develop a sense of awe at what they have to offer in terms of insights, compassion, and understanding. This is an interesting situation because we often think a community of one is a weaker place from which to graduate to a community of many and thereby gain strength. Often, an individual with a chronic illness can give a great deal of strength from within a community of one to the community of many.

Chapter 3

Finding the Strength Within: Accessing the Hidden Treasure of Our Spiritual Resources

DAN'S STORY OF SPIRITUAL CRISIS

Dan sat in a chair in a dark room, tears streaming down his face, paralyzed with shock and despair. He had no words to express the horrible situation with which he was being confronted. Dan and his wife, Emily, along with their two children, Sarah and David, had attended a community church for the past five years. Both Dan and Emily had been raised in a small Midwestern town where church was an integral part of the community and where church attendance was an important routine in many people's lives. They had expected to continue this tradition with their own family even though they had moved far from their hometown. They had even enrolled their children in the church's Christian academy where they were in the third and fifth grades. Dan and Emily had been proud to be members of this congregation and had supported the church with their time, money, and talents.

Then, two years ago, tragedy struck. Emily was driving David home from a soccer game when a drunk driver rammed into their minivan. David received only minor injuries, but Emily was killed instantly. Dan was devastated and depended heavily on the church for support to help him through that dark time. It seemed that every member of the church contributed to supporting him and the children in some way. Dan believed he and the children couldn't have survived without their help. A year later, he still felt deeply indebted to the church and was honored when the church board asked him to take on

Becoming Your Own Emotional Support System
Published by The Haworth Press, Inc., 2007. All rights reserved.
doi:10.1300/5828_03

a greater role in helping govern the church. It felt like a turning point for Dan; he would finally be able to give back to the church after being on the receiving end for such a long time.

Dan was a successful businessperson in the community and was highly respected for his ability to manage money and investments. The congregation had been growing and the church had identified a need for more space. Dan's advice was sought as the board considered putting an offer on a piece of property for a new building. Dan was flattered and eagerly agreed to look into the matter. It was the least he could do after all that was done for him and his kids. In Dan's mind, this was a wonderful opportunity to use the talents the Lord had given him. Subsequently, the chairman of the board gave Dan a detailed copy of the church's financial records so that he might do some research prior to helping negotiate the deal. At first, Dan thought that he was misreading the reports because he couldn't believe what he was seeing. The information in the reports didn't mesh at all with how he believed a church should financially conduct itself. Dan had high standards for himself in his business practices in the community and he had even higher standards for what he expected from his church.

All of the church property was listed in the pastor's name. Dan tried to rationalize this with all kinds of possible explanations. Many of these transactions had taken place before he joined the church, so maybe he just didn't know the history that would likely provide a reasonable explanation. He had always thought of the pastor as a strong, trustworthy leader, and this picture didn't fit the framework of the documents he had examined. It would only be Dan's second board meeting since joining the leadership group and he didn't want to come across as arrogant and condescending in his knowledge or as trying to meddle in something he didn't understand. Nevertheless, he needed some explanations and answers. Based on his research, Dan went with a list of questions and thoroughly expected to come home feeling silly about his doubts.

However, things did not happen that way at all. When Dan asked if he was missing some other documents with additional signatures of board members representing the church in the legal matter of church property ownership, he was told that he had all the pertinent documents. Dan then suggested that this was an unusual way to do business. Instantly, the looks Dan received from other board members made him wonder if he'd missed wiping off the last of the pizza sauce from dinner. The pastor jovially jumped in and said Dan was new to the board and so, obviously, he didn't understand the situation. He patiently and piously explained that since he was the one who was typically free during the week to go to the bank and conduct business, it just made sense that things should be in his name. That way, others wouldn't have to take time off of work for business transactions. This was actually a matter of considering others, an admirable Christian virtue, right?

Dan wasn't satisfied with this explanation, but let it drop. The subject of the new church property was introduced, incurring a discussion with how to proceed. For the first time, Dan got a good look at the location of the prospective property and the proposed development of a new facility. He immediately noticed that access to the new property wasn't very convenient to most of the congregation. He wondered out loud if others had considered that problem and were there any other alternatives?

Throats began to clear in a sea of dead silence. Again, the pastor, with his usual winning smile, spoke up and said that the problem had indeed been considered. However, the property actually belonged to his brother-in-law who needed to sell and therefore the church would be able to get it for an excellent price. Churches always have limited financial coffers and need to cut corners where they can, explained the pastor. Certainly Dan should be able to understand that.

Having more knowledge of property prices in the community than some of the other board members, Dan knew that the price wasn't all that good. He suggested that even a good price might not offset the difficulty most people would have with access or the extra expenses incurred in developing a lengthy entry from the main road.

Uncomfortable laughter filled the room and the pastor said, "What's the matter, Dan, don't you trust my judgment? Isn't this something, Dan's second time to a board meeting and already he seems to know more than all the rest of us combined even though we've been working on this project for months. We are obviously quite fortunate to have acquired a new member with so much quick wisdom."

Dan felt totally humiliated and embarrassed. He was in a silent state of shock for the rest of the meeting. Much of the shock came from the fact that the other board members didn't seem to blink an eye at the unethical nature of these dealings. In the past, Dan would have immediately gone home and run the experience past Emily who had always been quite perceptive. He was again reminded of the incredible vacuum her death had left in his life. He now had no one with whom to process the new light shed on a pastor he had always previously respected.

However, was the information really new and was it the only information indicating a problem? Maybe not. Dan had to admit to himself that he had been entertaining more and more concerns about the children's school. They had been coming home telling stories he hadn't wanted to believe. Being alone, some things were now just too overwhelming and he often pushed problems aside whenever possible in order to just get through the day. David had reported that Ms. Gail (the pastor's wife and principal of the school) had shamed him and Sarah in front of their friends. Apparently, about a month ago, David had encountered the wrath of Ms. Gail. He met a new boy at the YMCA who had just moved into the area with his family. They were Cambodians and were having a hard time making friends. David was overheard at school talking about his intention to invite his new friend to church. Ms. Gail told him it wouldn't be appropriate to do that since "those" people were too primitive to understand "our" faith. When David said he had always been taught by his father to be friendly to new kids, she told him that his father was obviously not mature enough in his faith to understand. David was confused, not wanting to get into further trouble for questioning his teacher, but also not wanting to hurt the feelings of his new friend.

Sarah had come home in tears only last week. She had worn her favorite dress to school. Dan knew the dress was a little short because Sarah had been growing the past year, but she was reluctant to put it aside. The dress had been a special gift from her mother, and Sarah always felt close to Emily when she wore it. Ms. Gail had told Sarah that only sluts wear skirts that short. Poor Sarah hadn't even known what slut meant. Ms. Gail had further remarked that since Sarah no longer had a mother someone from the church would need to instruct Dan on appropriate dress for young ladies. Sarah had burst into tears and ended up in the office. When Dan heard about the incident that evening, he had been furious at the insensitivity shown toward his daughter. He called Ms. Gail to determine whether these remarks had been true. Not only had they been accurate, but Ms. Gail had been extremely condescending and told Dan that his job was to parent and that he should let her handle the educating. Dan was shocked into silence at this response so he just hung up. He was busy preparing for the board meeting anyway and hadn't done any further follow-up at that time. The whole incident had left nagging doubts in the back of his mind, doubts that said things were not right and that he needed to address the issue at some point whether he wanted to or not. At the moment, Dan preferred to put it on a back shelf.

Dan belonged to a small study group at the church and eventually decided to share his concerns with them. He always valued the wisdom and friendships he found in this group and, when it was time for discussion, he unloaded. Afterward, the group became quiet. He interpreted this as concern and caring over the issues he disclosed. However, instead of the support he anticipated, Dan became the receiving end of pious smiles, gestures, and advice. He was told that the pastor and his wife were ordained to be in their roles and it was his duty to respect their positions of authority. In the group's opinion, Dan was slipping in his devotional life and was obviously becoming too lax in the discipline of his children. They wanted to be understanding in light of the loss of his wife, but now they felt it was their Christian duty to set Dan straight. According to group members, spreading doubts and rumors about the pastor and his wife were typical results of his failures. The last straw for Dan was the remark that this never would have happened if Emily were still alive.

Dan felt he had just entered the twilight zone and left the group as soon as possible, planning on the way home to leave the phone off the hook to forestall any further "advice." Dan thought that the loss of Emily was more than he could bear, but he had never doubted Emily's love and commitment to him, and that had seen him through. This was different. The very community he had relied on for support, guidance, and friendship had just betrayed everything he believed in. Even Dan's extended family had been kept in the background because the church took up so much time and energy. How could he go to them now when he had neglected those family relationships in favor of his fellow believers? The last thing he wanted to hear was "I told you so" from family who were not church-goers.

After disconnecting his phone other than for his own use, Dan began receiving a deluge of mail. Letters and notes expressed the condemnation, disappointment, and reprimands of his former friends and church leaders. He felt surrounded by an unknown enemy, seeing no possible routes of escape and seeing no one who might validate his experience. Dan removed his children from the school and enrolled them in public school, even though he and Emily had always valued and wanted a private school education for their children. After what he had recently undergone, he no longer doubted the validity of his children's school experiences. He could no longer tolerate seeing David and Sarah come home from school crying because of the teasing, taunting, and scapegoating to which they were being exposed.

This all seemed so bizarre. Dan still held onto his faith and didn't want to give the church a negative face in front of his non–church-going friends, who were quite few anyway. He also felt that no one would ever believe that such behavior and treatment could go on in a well-respected community church. Dan considered going to a different church but hesitated. He didn't want to answer questions as to why he wanted to change churches. If he told the truth, he felt he wouldn't be believed and he certainly couldn't lie. Dan also had to admit that there were times when he wondered if it really was he who had somehow gotten off track. He had no one with whom he could talk to about the situation and was sinking into depression. Dan was lost and needed to consider creating a community of one.

DAN'S NEED FOR A COMMUNITY OF ONE

What specifically placed Dan in need of a community of one? First, Dan was already withdrawn due to grief over the death of his wife. His role in life had recently changed and he hadn't yet adjusted to that unexpected change. Because of that, he felt awkward questioning or challenging people whom previously provided emotional support and friendship. Also, Dan hadn't yet developed new friendships that reflected his current status as a single dad. He had allowed himself to belong to a group that, due to his grief, he didn't evaluate as thoroughly as he would have otherwise. He enjoyed belonging without making sure the situation was healthy, balanced, and a reflection of his very genuine spiritual beliefs.

Dan was flattered and proud that the church respected his talents and abilities in the secular world. Perhaps some of that pride initially blinded him to the questionable situation in which he found himself. He rightly judged that giving to others and finding productive ways to use his free time would help in his grief over Emily's death. After the first several months of intense grief, he needed to move on and wanted to do that in a productive way. Dan was a very smart man, certainly not naive to the ways of the world and what people often do for self-gain. He just never expected this pursuit of self-gain to be rooted in his local church.

Finally, in his state of neediness, he took his eyes off his own genuine faith, which had previously been a satisfying basis for his course in life. Dan was allowing others to dictate what his faith should be and how he should live out that faith. Dan's faith was becoming horizontal in nature, based on comparisons with others rather than vertical in nature, where God Himself determined the essence of faith. Dan accepted at face value, without checking, the beliefs of others, assuming they were in line with his own beliefs.

THE TARNISHING OF SPIRITUAL RESOURCES

Dan's experience is not as unusual as one might first suppose. We have all been confronted with many instances in the media in which spiritual leaders have demonstrated their human failings. Many people view their spiritual beliefs as some of their most precious values. In fact, spiritual beliefs go so deep as to help us explain our origins and purpose for life. This is true whether we're talking about Christianity, Buddhism, Hinduism, Judaism, or any of a multitude of spiritual belief systems. Our spirituality is often the place we go to when all else fails, when we need answers about the mysteries and disappointments of life. When people encounter problems in their lives, they frequently go to their spiritual leaders for advice and direction even before they seek out a professional counselor. For many, if you can't trust your pastor, your rabbi, or your priest, whom can you trust?

This had been Dan's perspective. His spiritual beliefs and the associated connections with his pastor and church were the foundation of what he found meaningful in life. When he discovered that the spiritual leaders he had trusted and depended on had misused their authority for their own gain, he was devastated. He didn't know where else to turn for help and hadn't even felt so alone when Emily died. At least with Emily's death, he had been surrounded with support. When the ugly truth about the church and school was exposed, Dan lost his friends, his support system, his confidence in what he believed was right, and the stable underpinnings upon which he had based his life. Dan had to re-examine his spirituality from square one and now had no one he trusted to help him with the process. He was now reduced to needing to develop a community of one.

Power is an important commodity to many people and people in churches are often no different. The consequences resulting from these power plays can be devastating. Ronald Enroth (1992) stated,

> Unlike physical abuse that often results in bruised bodies, spiritual and pastoral abuse leaves scars on the psyche and soul. It is inflicted by persons who are accorded respect and honor in our society by virtue of their role as religious leaders and models of spiritual authority. (p. 29)

How right he is! Because our spiritual beliefs are often so deep-seated and our respect for spiritual leadership often so elevated, when behaviors don't match our beliefs, we are crushed.

Enroth goes on to say, "The perversion of power that we see in abusive churches disrupts and divides families, fosters an unhealthy dependence of members on the leadership, and creates, ultimately, spiritual confusion in the lives of victims" (p. 29). David Johnson and Jeff VanVonderen (1991) describe the same dynamic when they say,

> The first characteristic of an abusive religious system is what we call power-posturing. Power-posturing simply means that leaders spend a lot of time focused on their own authority and reminding others of it, as well. This is necessary because their spiritual authority isn't real—based on genuine godly character—it is postured. (p. 63)

This is exactly what Dan experienced and it resulted in his needing to build a community of one.

This might seem like a very harsh perspective of spiritual leaders, and in all fairness, it is doubtful that most spiritual leaders start out with a masterfully planned power trip. Many who have succumbed to the temptation of power fell into the pattern gradually and over time. Being in spiritual leadership is an intoxicating experience. The entire church system is set up to revere spiritual leaders, often seeing them on a higher plane, as examples to be followed no matter what, and believed to be the very representatives of God Himself. Although spiritual leaders are indeed placed in positions of authority over their constituents, and may have special training, knowledge, gifts, and talents to perform this function, they are still human beings, accountable to God as are we all. True leadership based on godly character is a humbling position, a position of service to others and not a platform to elevate oneself.

Individuals such as Dan who have experienced significant loss, abuse, or are otherwise damaged provide an easy target for a power-minded leader to use. Dan suddenly found himself in a lonely role, that of a single dad who was confused and lost in his new single adult identity as well.

In 1991, Stephen Arterburn and Jack Felton wrote this about people caught up in the belonging offered through a faith system, "Rational thought and objective evaluation are discarded to enjoy the emotional rush that comes from breaking out of isolation and joining others in spiritual pursuit" (p. 132). After losing his beloved wife, Dan felt like a new baby cuddled in his mother's arms when he found acceptance and belonging in his church, a place where he could be served and could also serve others. It seemed to be just what he needed to begin his healing journey. Many churches would offer just that. Unfortunately, in his grief, Dan did give up his "rational thought and objective evaluation" of the situation until he was once again faced with deep hurt and loss.

RESPONSES TO SITUATIONS OF SPIRITUAL CRISIS THAT LEAD TO CREATING A COMMUNITY OF ONE

Dan had been caught in his vulnerability. The real danger for Dan was if he translated this experience to all churches. If he allowed this to happen, he would deny himself the opportunity to find true spiritual support in a healthy environment. For Dan, building a community of one would involve regaining his spiritual bearings and then learning how to distinguish a healthy church from which he could gain the support he needed from an unhealthy or abusive church. According to Johnson and VanVonderen (1991),

> There is no test to diagnose spiritual abuse. There are only spiritual clues: lack of joy in the Christian life; tiredness from trying hard to measure up; disillusionment about God and spiritual things; uneasiness, lack of trust, or even fear of those who care

about "God" things, even legitimately; a profound sense of missing your best Friend; cynicism or grief over good news that turned out to be too good to be true. (p. 194)

If Dan had known these clues, he likely wouldn't have found himself in search of a community of one.

In creating a community of one, we must discover the truth of who we are, where we come from, and our purpose in life. This will involve becoming acquainted with our Creator. God never minds an honest search for truth. In fact, He likely enjoys it. Questions such as: Why am I here? What's my purpose in life? Where is my life going? Is there a reason for suffering? are all legitimate things we wonder about. Rick Warren writes (2002), "In the Bible, the friends of God were honest about their feelings, often complaining, second-guessing, accusing, and arguing with their Creator. God, however, didn't seem to be bothered by this frankness; in fact, he encouraged it" (p. 93). God can handle our questions, our concerns, our grief, and our problems. Based on a developing connection with our Creator, we can become acquainted with our deepest selves as well.

When it comes to truth, we often accept the fact that God is truth. We accept that we should be truthful, and then we fudge the truth to suit our needs. Fudging the truth may extend all the way from telling white lies, to stretching the truth, to outright lies. Brennan Manning (2005) states,

> The first step in the pursuit of truth is not the moral resolution to avoid the habit of petty lying—however unattractive a character disfigurement that may be. It is not the decision to stop deceiving others. It is the decision to stop deceiving ourselves. Unless we have the same relentless passion for the truth that Jesus exhibited in the temple, we are undermining our faith, betraying the Lord, and deceiving ourselves. Self-deception is the enemy of wholeness because it prevents us from seeing ourselves as we really are. It covers up our lack of growth in the Spirit of the truthful One and keeps us from coming to terms with our real personalities. (p. 4)

As painful as it might be, we can never come to a place of personal peace within a community of one if we're not completely truthful with ourselves.

As Manning says, self-deception is the enemy of wholeness, and wholeness is exactly what we are trying to achieve in creating a community of one. Lying to ourselves and about ourselves has likely contributed to our needing a community of one in the first place. Certainly, an avoidance of the truth has brought us to this end. Avoiding the truth allows our fears to get out of hand, our anxieties to take on monstrous proportions, and our relationships to become distorted. Dan had to come to terms with the truth as he created his community of one—truth about God, about himself, and about those in the community of many with whom he had associated.

Chapter 4

The Truth About the Royal Family: Stigmas Can Make Finding Support a Challenge

MAGGIE'S STORY OF SEXUAL ABUSE

Maggie sat comfortably in her chaise lounge by the pool in her backyard. It was late afternoon and she was sipping a glass of white wine, physically relaxing while at the same time continuing to experience emotional chaos. The incongruence of her life sometimes made it so difficult to function that she just had to check out for a while. Maggie wryly thought she could easily qualify to work as a field agent for the CIA. She had lived a double life for many years and believed no one suspected a thing. Maggie was thirty-six years old, raised in an upper middle-class family. She had graduated from a well-respected eastern university and had married Jake, four years her senior, who now provided for a successful upper middle-class family of their own. He worked hard and his future in the high-tech field seemed secure. Their two children, Hannah and Aaron, enjoyed even more privileges than Maggie had as a child.

Maggie closed her eyes and began to wonder how much longer she could maintain her double facade of a socially confident wife and mother co-existing with a frightened, abused child. The very act of closing her eyes seemed to invite once again those horrid memories that she fought to keep hidden. It had all started when she was five years old and her sister, Ellie, was three. Her father's sales business had just started taking off and he was putting in long hours. A large part of his success depended on networking and socially interacting with potential clients. "Uncle Ed" was an important client of her fa-

Becoming Your Own Emotional Support System
Published by The Haworth Press, Inc., 2007. All rights reserved.
doi:10.1300/5828_04

ther and they began to spend a lot of time together. They golfed, played tennis, and sailed, all their activities involving alcohol to one extent or another. It seemed her father always deferred to Uncle Ed, and even as a young child Maggie despised her father's weak nature.

Helene, Maggie's mother, was always emotionally distant. Once, Maggie remembered overhearing some women at an afternoon tea refer to her mother as a "cold fish" behind her back. Maggie had to concur it was an accurate description. Oh, Helene made sure that Maggie and Ellie went to dance class, piano lessons, and later on, etiquette classes. She had done her duty of making sure they would be prepared to be socially appropriate at all times. However, Maggie could never recall hugs, kisses, or the soft comforting voice of an emotionally available mother. She had wondered what it would be like to have a mother who would snuggle and giggle under the covers, sharing little girl secrets. Later on, Maggie realized her father must have also missed those loving qualities her mother lacked. Her parents' relationship was hard to understand. Who knows? Maybe her strong mother also despised her weak father. Or maybe her mother wasn't so strong herself. Maggie had never pretended to have it figured out. However, these types of realizations came in her kinder moments, which were quite fleeting.

The secrets and snuggles she did get were not those she had dreamed about and they developed instead into her worst nightmares. At first, she felt unbelievably special. She would hear her parents arguing in their bedroom late at night and when the loud voices stopped she would shortly begin to feel her father snuggling in her bed. Nothing more happened in those early years. She felt like a queen, knowing that she was the one person her father came to for comfort when her mother had upset him with her coldness and anger. Finally, someone recognized her need for closeness as well. A mutually beneficial relationship, or so she thought. At times, Maggie wondered why Ellie wasn't included in these snuggling sessions. She and Ellie were very close. On the other hand, she enjoyed the special attention she received from her father and didn't want to jeopardize it by including Ellie. Ellie always seemed to be Helene's favorite anyway, so it wasn't like she was really missing out on anything.

And then Uncle Ed entered the scene. That also seemed quite innocent in the beginning. When Maggie was eight, Uncle Ed and her father began taking her with them on their golf games, their little "caddy princess." Others on the golf course would stop and comment how nice it was of her father to include his daughter in his leisure activities and spend so much time with her. Uncle Ed also developed a proprietary air about her, putting his arm around her shoulders and giving her a hug with every successful shot. Maggie loved the attention and certainly preferred this to the critical eye and often cold reception she received from Helene. It was funny how she never felt comfortable calling Helene "mommy" or "mom." It was "mother" at best and often "Helene" with a disrespectful tone in private. But with her father and Uncle Ed, Maggie was part of the group and enjoyed the envy of Ellie and her friends whose fathers often engaged in their male leisure activities without their children.

Uncle Ed and her father always stopped to get her ice cream after their golf game. Vanilla almond crunch was her favorite and they never disappointed her. It was odd how those little details were still so fresh. Anymore, Maggie avoided anything with the word vanilla in it.

Uncle Ed moved the touching beyond a proprietary hug when Maggie was about nine. It always happened when her father's head was turned away. From her adult perspective, she wondered if it happened the other way around, that her father would turn his head when Uncle Ed began traveling. After all, Uncle Ed was one of her father's most lucrative accounts. It was a perfectly horrid thought. Eventually, Maggie felt like the fringe benefit in her father's business dealings with Uncle Ed. And that was a perfectly horrid feeling. Maggie began dreading the golf games, the ice cream shop, and everything else about Uncle Ed and her father.

Maggie's thirteenth birthday began with a party for her and her friends from school. Helene went all out, hiring a band, caterers, and a professional photographer to capture the festivities. Maggie suspected the photographer was actually hired to obtain just the right shot for the society page in the newspaper. Although Maggie's birthday was in July, there was not much warmth in Helene's "Happy Birthday" greeting. While Maggie and her friends enjoyed themselves, Helene and Maggie's father entertained guests of their own, including Uncle Ed. Maggie's friends began leaving after ten p.m. and when they were all gone, she went to say goodnight to her parents and their guests. She noticed that the adults were beginning to slur their words after too much alcohol, so she was glad to be going to bed. She had received some wonderful gifts and had enjoyed the time with her friends immensely. Maggie didn't want this special event in her life ruined by hanging around with drunken adults.

Maggie was exhausted and just about to slip into sweet dreams of being a teenager when she heard footsteps outside her door. The next thing she knew, Uncle Ed had shut her door and was standing by her bed. He leaned down and whispered in her ear, "Maggie, it's the perfect time now to teach you all that it means to grow up." After that night, Maggie never wanted to be a grown-up again. From that point on, it was all about forgetting. Maggie tried just about everything to help her forget—alcohol, drugs, sex, even diving into academics at one point. All these things only helped temporarily and then the nightmares returned. Every time a door creaked, Maggie tensed in fear, waiting for her living nightmare to return. As an adult, Maggie would tell herself this was ridiculous, but nevertheless being on guard became a way of life.

Finally, in her later teen years Maggie decided that entering a life of make-believe was the only way to survive. She was very aware that she had been setting a negative example for Ellie and genuinely felt remorseful for that. At least living in a world of make-believe gave her something in common with Helene. Maggie shocked herself with that thought. She never believed she and Helene would have anything in common. Dan Allender (1990) discusses this desire to protect oneself.

> [A] commitment never to be hurt again by the abuser (or anyone else like him) creates a hard, inflexible exterior and, in turn, leads to the loneliness that the hardness was developed to avoid. The victim's defensive armor will add more pain to her soul and her pain will strengthen her resolve never to be hurt, inevitably increasing the wintery ice in her heart. The protection against pain, in fact, intensifies the pain that it was supposed to decrease. (p. 40)

Although Maggie had never wanted to feel the coldness she saw in Helene, she seemed completely unable to escape it. It led her to wonder about what might have been in Helene's past and for the first time, she felt a glimmer of sympathy for her mother.

Now, however, make-believe was taking too much energy. Besides, watching her own children was causing her to realize all that she had missed in her own childhood. Maggie had to admit she was lonely. Make-believe had helped her attract a successful husband, but at the same time, prevented the development of a truly intimate relationship. She didn't really know Jake except for things such as his preferred drink, what suit he liked to wear to certain events, and which clients she needed to impress for him. He certainly didn't know her. Maggie was very fearful that if Jake knew the truth of what had happened to her, he would deem her no longer good enough and divorce her quickly. She worried a lot that Jake would see her as tainted goods. In reality, there was no evidence for this. Jake had always treated her kindly and clearly adored their kids.

Nevertheless, if she had learned nothing else from her childhood, she had learned not to trust the people closest to her. Maggie felt different, dirty, and in many ways, an outcast. She longed for personal connections, craved legitimate affection, and had a strong need to give these things as well. She was also terrified and clueless as to how to accomplish any of that. Dan Allender (1990) asks us to

> Consider the damage done to the soul when the abuse is fused with the legitimate longings of the heart. The flower of deep longing for love is somehow hideously intertwined with the weed of abuse. Longings are wed to abuse, abuse begets shame, and shame is inextricably related to a hatred for one's own hungry soul. Any significant abuse causes the victim to despise the way he or she's been made: a person wired for deep, satisfying, eternal involvement with others and God. (p. 49)

Maggie's deepest desire was to be part of a community of many. First, however, she needed to become a community of one.

MAGGIE'S NEED FOR A COMMUNITY OF ONE

One might ask, why would someone like Maggie need to develop a community of one? Why couldn't she just immediately access the community of many? Maggie, unlike many others, certainly had the financial resources to tap into all sorts of supportive networks. Why couldn't she just go to therapy to deal with the past abuse issues? These are legitimate questions. There are many people who might even feel resentful of all that Maggie has in terms of material possessions, even though they would admit the pain of her past was a genuine and terrible burden to bear. They might say that the fur coat in Maggie's closet would surely give her plenty of comforting feelings. In all likelihood, Maggie had said all these things to herself. She had sensed the envy and jealousy of others over her successful status in life. She often felt guilty, undeserving of help because of all the things she had. Even though Maggie had material resources, the truth was that her shame, confusion, and poor self-esteem kept her as much in a state of poverty as the proverbial skid row bum.

Although the shame Maggie felt was really not hers to carry, she did carry it on behalf of her mother, her father, and Uncle Ed. In terms of emotional responsibility, the perpetrators were getting away with murder—Maggie's emotional murder! Maggie often felt such a load of shame that she felt unworthy of life. In earlier years, this had led her down many self-destructive paths, but she then learned to deaden her soul instead. At least the consequences of a deadened soul seemed easier. There was less public exposure and therefore, fewer negative public reactions with which to contend. However, her deadened soul very effectively kept her from the personal connections she longed for in the community of many. From Maggie's distorted perspective, the people in the community of many were so above her in every way that she felt she had no right to even consider connections. Her basic assumption was that if they knew the truth of her abusive past, they would heap just as much blame on her as on Helene, her father, and Uncle Ed. Her shame served as a six-foot concrete barrier from the community of many of which she wanted to become a member.

Also needing to be dealt with was Maggie's constant state of confusion. Since toddlerhood, her memories were filled with comments from significant people in her life that she was worthless, she got what she deserved, she should have been more like her cute little sister Ellie, she should be more appreciative of all they had done for her, and so forth. To have any thought that these comments were not true meant that these important people, mostly family, had lied to her. However, they could not lie, because Maggie had to trust them to care for her. It must really be her fault, just as they said. If she tried harder things would be better. She did try harder, as hard as she could, to do pleasing things, but only received unpleasing remarks about her "failures."

Christine Courtois (1988), in her groundbreaking book on incest, describes a series of messages or rules that family members must follow in order to protect the family secret. These rules are as follows:

> Don't feel. Keep your feelings in check. Do not show your feelings, especially anger. Be in control at all times. Do not show weakness. Do not ask for help. Deny what is really happening. Disbelieve your own senses/perceptions. Lie to yourself and to others. Don't trust yourself or anyone else. No one is trustworthy. Keep the secret. If you tell you will not be believed and it will not get help. Be ashamed of yourself. You are to blame for everything. (p. 45)

Maggie knew these rules well and had grown up in an emotional double bind of awesome magnitude. Combined with the outside facade of financial and social success that her family maintained, the result was that Maggie's thinking was a mess.

Finally, Maggie's low self-esteem led her to believe that the great blessing of her life was to be allowed to live at all. She saw herself as one of the lowest human beings on the planet, in spite of her Donna Karan wardrobe. Why should she not think these things? No one would treat their daughter, their beloved oldest daughter, the way she had been treated. She knew from being a mother herself that the abuse was not natural. The only logical conclusion in Maggie's mind was that she must be a defective human being. Helene didn't treat Ellie like a non-person. As far as Maggie knew, Ellie was not abused by Uncle Ed. There had to be something horrendously, drastically wrong with Maggie herself. From Maggie's perspective, it was ridiculous to think anything else. All of these things combined to lead Maggie into a distorted tangle of thoughts resulting in emotional imprisonment. There was no way she could jump from her emotionally impoverished state into a community of many without first constructing a community of one.

THE ISOLATING EFFECTS OF SEXUAL ABUSE

Unfortunately, Maggie's story is common among victims of sexual abuse. Part of Maggie's isolation occurred because her abusers, her father and Uncle Ed, were people that she should have been able to trust unquestionably. She also felt betrayed by her mother, who did not protect her. Lenore Walker (1994) has been a prolific writer on the subject of sexual abuse. She speaks eloquently about this combination of violated trust and the resulting isolation.

> When humans are young, their world often revolves around their parents. Parents are the source of safety and security, of love and understanding, of nurturance and support. Incest violates the trust that is at the heart of the child's relationship with the world. Any attempt by the incest victim to reorganize her understanding of and relationship to her world when this violation occurs may be far beyond her cognitive-affective abilities. Rather than experience the cognitive paralysis or disintegration that threatens to occur when her world is disrupted to this extent, the child simply isolates each abusive event, psychologically wraps it in a sort of cognitive cocoon, and begins not to see it. The denial enables her life to continue, although this movement forward comes at a tremendous cost. (p. 231)

Maggie moved forward, seemingly with glamour and success, but the cost to her was isolation of her true self, an inability to be authentic even with her own husband and children.

Many sexual abuse victims have a distinct feeling of being "different." They may or may not be able to put their finger on precisely what makes them different, but it's tangibly there. Some of the symptoms of sexual abuse, particularly incest, as E. Sue Blume describes (1990), may help explain this. Characteristics such as night terrors and an extreme need for privacy may cause children or even adults to avoid staying over at someone else's home. There may be a desire to wear lots of baggy clothing, even when the weather dictates no need for it. Resulting comments may lead a person to simply stay at home. The development of eating disorders is common and may make sharing meals with others agonizing. Abuse victims tend to be overly solemn and humorless. Why are they not laughing, isn't this joke hilarious? They are not the life of the party. On the other hand, they might be the poster girl of parties, the one always up for a good time, albeit way overdone. An inability to set limits and appropriate boundaries with others may lead victims to be taken advantage of and/or to lose respectful treatment by others. Sexual problems of all varieties are common and in a society where so much emphasis is placed on elite sexual performance, victims can feel completely lacking and out of synch. The list could go on, but it is easy to see why a sexual abuse victim might feel isolated and reluctant to join a community of many.

Styles of relating are an issue addressed by Dan Allender (1990). He states,

> Although *obvious* (emphasis mine) secondary symptoms of sexual abuse are not always present, past damage will inevitably show itself in one's style of relating to others. . . . A relational style is the "typical" way of protecting oneself in contact with other people. Self-protection is, in essence, the commitment to never be hurt again, to never be powerless, betrayed, or ambivalent in the way we once were. (p. 155)

Secondary symptoms, such as those described by E. Sue Blume, lead to a sense of confusion and uncertainty about how to relate to others as there is no reference point as to what is normal and usually very little trust to ask others. Women, such as Maggie, who grow up to have children of their own often parent out of a fantasy world they wish they themselves had.

RESPONSES TO SEXUAL ABUSE THAT LEAD TO CREATING A COMMUNITY OF ONE

It is not always financial poverty that keeps people from accessing helpful resources. Poverty of the self and the soul are powerful deterrents that can prevent one from accessing resources. This was true for Maggie. Her self-concept in general was a barrier that kept her from reaching out, but there was also the issue of her not trusting anyone. Maggie learned from her family and close family friends that no one is trustworthy. This was so indelibly printed on her mind that she had never wondered if it was false; it had to be true because of her experience. Although Jake might have been very kind, understanding, and encouraging, Maggie had never dared share her pain. He was her husband, someone so close to her that she could not trust he had her best interests at heart. That's what she learned from her own family of origin. Those closest to you are the ones most likely to betray you. There was so much to lose if she risked herself and her fears were proven true. What if she did take a risk and trusted Jake with the truth of her past? The stigma of her being a sexual abuse victim might be more than he could handle. Her father had taught her that business success was more important that anything, even his daughter's innocence.

What could possibly motivate someone in Maggie's frame of mind to consider making life changes? Possibly her own pain would become so overwhelming that she would be compelled to reach out in order to survive. More likely, someone she loved would need her to be in a better place than she was, such as her children. Many reasons exist for sexual abuse survivors to arrive at needing to create a community of one. Sometimes, there are few memories of the abuse, or the memories have been greatly minimized. There's simply a sense that something's wrong, not right, not what it could be or should be; there is a need to fix—"something." Perhaps he or she has been depressed or anxious for a long time and nothing has seemed to help. Or, the eating disorder is failing to keep unwanted feelings stuffed or the cutting behavior is no longer enough to let all the pain out—these are things that often lead people to recognize the need to create a community of one.

The biggest risk for sexual abuse survivors as they decide whether or not to create a community of one is the risk of allowing themselves to feel alive. Can they allow themselves the little tingles, the thrills, the heart quivers, the sinking feelings, the welling up of tears, the release as the tears flow down their cheeks, the total awe of having a full assortment of emotions at their fingertips, ready to be used whenever needed? This translates into becoming no mere survivor—slithering and slinking around trying to work up the nerve to begin a community of one. It translates into being a conqueror, head held high, eager to move forward into a community of one and then a community of many.

Chapter 5

Cleaning House: Identifying
the Unnecessary and Letting It Go

TERRY'S STORY OF ADHD AND JOB LOSS

Terry struggled all through school. In fact, as a kid, it was torture to have to wake up in the morning and show up in a classroom. He remembered endless nagging, yelling, bribery, and frustration by his parents as they tried to get him to comply with a schedule. By age seven, Terry's parents wondered if something was wrong with their son and took him to a psychologist for an evaluation. Terry was diagnosed with ADHD, attention deficit hyperactivity disorder, combined type. Combined type meant Terry had symptoms of both inattention and hyperactivity. Although Terry's parents were assured that he was of at least average intelligence and maybe slightly above, he had a hard time accessing that intelligence due to problems with sitting still and focusing on his studies. From second grade on, Terry saw his parents' disappointment whenever it was report card time. They tried not to show it, but to Terry, they might as well have put a neon sign in the window saying "Our son Terry is a failure."

Terry also endured endless teasing from peers. "Why can't you sit still, do you have ants in your pants?" "How stupid can you be?" "Why do you have to talk so loud?" From teachers, he heard: "You could understand this if you just tried a little harder." "Why can't you just relax and stop bothering the other kids?" "Go to the office if you can't behave!" Terry knew he had tried as hard as he could to "not bother people" and to please his parents. Things got a little easier once the psychologist diagnosed the problem and recommended his parents have him evaluated for medication management of the ADHD. His pediatrician had experience with ADHD and started him

Becoming Your Own Emotional Support System
Published by The Haworth Press, Inc., 2007. All rights reserved.
doi:10.1300/5828_05

on medication. Even then, Terry worried about when the medication wore off and wondered what people thought of someone who had to take pills just to function. He also felt he had to hide the fact that he took medication because the other kids teased him enough as it was.

Eventually, Terry was placed in classes for special-needs kids which further stigmatized him with his peers. He had a tutor who helped him with the more tedious subjects such as math and grammar. Terry's friendships were limited, basically consisting of other misfits at school. He had tried alcohol and marijuana in high school thinking it might even help with the ADHD, but instead of helping, it only left him feeling more disregulated. He was afraid of getting into trouble with the law anyway. Terry's parents were as supportive as they could be, always encouraging him to do his best. Terry graduated from high school determined to make his parents proud of him as an adult. His grades weren't good enough for college and frankly, the thought of more English classes with all that reading was more than he could tolerate. With some maturity under his belt and some strategies he gained in a brief course of therapy, Terry believed he could succeed in a technical school. He graduated with a certificate in computer technology and was on his way.

Terry and his parents were relieved that he made it to adulthood and now had a skill to support himself. Terry was personable, hardworking, and quickly found employment at a high-tech company on the East coast close to family and friends. Within a few years, Terry established himself as a good worker and met a secretary, Nancy, who also worked there. Nancy had such a sweet disposition that Terry overcame his social reluctance and asked her out. They dated for a year, married, and began a family of their own. Nancy seemed to have the patience to deal with Terry's symptoms when they slipped through his meds and all seemed well. Although Terry did not make a high-end salary, he made enough for Nancy to stay home with their children, which was an important value to both of them. There was little extra to put in a savings account, but they didn't worry all that much because they felt that Terry's job was secure. His advancement in the company had been steady, though certainly not stellar.

Terry's ADHD problems had remained into adulthood and he felt he had learned to manage them fairly well. Evaluations at work typically stated "needs better organization skills," "could benefit from a time management course," and "co-workers often feel they are not listened to." In spite of these comments, Terry was well liked by his managers and co-workers.

After eight years with the company, no one was more shocked than Terry when he was laid off due to a downsizing trend in the company. Terry was told that, although he was a valued employee, there were others who had been with the company equally as long with better skills. The management rhetoric was not very comforting to Terry. It took him back to high school, and even before, when he had tried so hard to please his teachers and parents with his work and never felt he measured up.

Nancy was supportive but also worried about Terry finding a new job. Both were well aware of the tight job market as well as the deficits resulting from the ADHD which Terry fought constantly. Terry was offered a reasonable severance package and they knew they would be all right financially for a few months. Hopefully, those few months were all they would need. Although certainly discouraged, Terry saw this as a bump in the road and felt he would soon be back on track. Initially, he framed the loss of his job to friends and family as a matter of being the low man on the totem pole. He brushed it off as a common occurrence in the computer field and likely a blessing in disguise, as it would afford him the opportunity to look for something better. He would say anything to cover his fear of criticism and expressed disappointments. Terry internalized any problems as personal defects and underneath his rosy presentation, he felt humiliated and defeated.

Terry made contact with a recruiter, posted his resume with job search engines on the Internet, and began filling out applications. He went on a few interviews but nothing panned out. The jobs were either entry-level positions that didn't pay enough to meet his financial obligations or he didn't have the appropriate training. Terry realized that having only a technical school certificate put him at a disadvantage in the job market, but with his learning problems, he had felt lucky to achieve that. The thought of getting further education crossed his mind but in the end he felt the obstacles were insurmountable. Even if he could be accepted into another training program with his mediocre school history, financing would put a tremendous strain on his family. Nancy was supportive, but only to a point. Besides, class work filled him with such anxiety that he didn't know if his mental health could handle it.

Meanwhile, the bills kept coming. Terry and Nancy's children, Randy and Nate, were now five and six years old and beginning school. Already they were seeing signs in their two young sons of possible learning disabilities. Remembering what he had gone through, Terry felt responsible and guilty, believing he had passed along these problems to his two sons whom he loved dearly. Testing, tutoring, and counseling also meant more money would be required to meet their needs. Their oldest son, Nate, was also beginning to exhibit some behavior problems and Nancy was feeling stretched to capacity trying to manage the boys. Terry tried to help with the boys, but at times his guilt led him to feel inept and he would just check out, leaving it to Nancy. He knew this wasn't fair to her but he could feel himself slipping more and more into a state of depression, withdrawing from Nancy, friends, and extended family.

With only a month left on the severance package and no prospects in sight, Terry began to feel desperate. Nancy's anxieties were being expressed as anger toward Terry. She felt he just wasn't organized enough or persistent enough in his search. Nancy didn't realize she was reiterating the kinds of remarks he had heard all his life. Even though they had always gotten along fairly well, they now began a pattern of constant bickering, with the bickering more frequently breaking out into verbal fights. In the midst of this family tension, Nate's behavioral problems escalated. The situation was untenable and Terry finally took advantage of a career counselor's services that were provided by his former company. Terry was advised to widen his job search to the West coast where there were more opportunities in the high-tech industry. Terry presented this option to Nancy and although they had hoped to remain on the East coast with family and friends, they realized it might be necessary for their family's financial survival. Anything seemed better than their current situation.

Terry again sent out an avalanche of resumes and within the month was rewarded with a job offer in northern California. The pay wasn't great and the cost of living was just as high as the East coast, but they were out of money and Terry felt that once he was in the area he might find other opportunities. Nancy agreed and they packed up their belongings and the kids, said their good-byes, and were off. Initially, they were thankful that Terry had a job and the cross-country trip seemed like a great adventure for their family. They were determined to accept their situation with the most positive attitude they could muster. On their arrival they discovered their start-up apartment wasn't what they had hoped for. The neighborhood seemed a little rough and they didn't feel it was safe to let the boys out to play without supervision. However, it was all they could afford on Terry's salary. They reasoned that once the boys had settled in school, Nancy might have to go back to work so they could afford better living accommodations. The pressures of losing his job, worrying about money, having to move across country, and leaving family and friends shifted to the pressures of adjusting to a new job, a new environment, and no supports.

Transitions had always been hard for Terry and now they were also hard for the boys. There were calls from the school almost immediately regarding the boys' negative behaviors. With the additional stressors in the family, Randy was also expressing his frustrations behaviorally. Terry understood the difficulties and pressures his sons were experiencing; he'd been there himself. Nevertheless, discipline was necessary and hard to enforce. Nancy found a secretarial position but resented it, feeling she had had to compromise her mothering role against her will. Co-workers were courteous to Terry and tried to be helpful, but they were not as friendly as his old group and Terry's lack of self-confidence made it difficult to get to know them.

Nancy's resentment and anger were hard to miss, so Terry felt he had no support there either. He was regretfully seeing a side of Nancy he hadn't known existed. During this time of testing she had shown a selfish side, a side that hated compromise, and a side that seemed to need more from Terry than he was capable of giving. He could acknowledge that she was under just as much stress as he was, but his expectations of their marriage had been that they would be pillars of strength for one another in times of adversity. The reality was that Nancy's pillar was more like a bamboo pole blowing in the strong winds. It didn't mean that he wanted to give up on his marriage, far from it. However, the disappointment ran deep. And it was the loss of a support system he had assumed would always be present and available.

His depression deepened and he began to feel hopeless about his future and his ability to provide well for his family. He couldn't sleep, he began losing weight, and the enjoyment in life was gone. Terry began having nightmares where his worries of being jobless expanded to his whole family living on the streets in tattered clothes, rummaging through the garbage cans for food, and having to fend off thieves and beggars who didn't want to share their territory or that of their allies. Terry recognized that his imagination was going beyond wild, but he still found it hard to shake the feelings of desperation and hopelessness after waking up from these horrible dreams. Terry withdrew, isolating himself both physically and emotionally, merely trying to survive and feeling lousy about even that. It was most definitely time that Terry learned what it meant to create a community of one.

TERRY'S NEED FOR A COMMUNITY OF ONE

Terry had fallen into the trap of self-hatred. He felt he couldn't do anything right. Not only that, Terry believed everyone around him also felt he couldn't do anything right. There was no solid evidence of that, but Terry believed it nonetheless. In his book titled *A Glimpse of Jesus* (2003), Brennan Manning focuses on this whole issue of self-hatred. He says,

> Self-hatred stands as an insuperable obstacle to growth and maturity. It derails interaction with others and renders us impotent to give or receive love. The self-condemning memory selects only negative recollections. Previous kindnesses and thoughtful gestures are perceived as vitiated by self-seeking. All other emotions are blocked out, and a sense of personal worthlessness prevails. We become more closed, less communicative, less comfortable to be around. If prevailed upon to speak, we express deep disappointment at our lack of spiritual progress and dwell on the unlikelihood of future improvement. Caring for others is existentially impossible because we cannot be compassionate toward ourselves. (pp. 134-135)

Although Nancy was indeed feeling angry and stressed, she genuinely loved Terry and believed that things would get better in time. Hiding out in this cloak of self-hatred, Terry couldn't believe that even when Nancy shared with him her hopes for the future and her continuing love.

Terry was in desperate need of developing a community of one, but as Brennan described, his self-hatred was an obstacle that kept him from being compassionate even toward himself. The negative memories that reminded him of his struggles in school flooded his mind, allowing no room for positive thinking, forward planning, or encouraging input from others.

> Most adults with ADD have suffered years of feeling demoralized, discouraged, and ineffective due to a history of frustrations and failures in school, work, family, and/or social domains. Many are plagued with a chronic inner sense of underachievement and intense frustration. Moreover, many have repeatedly heard negative messages about themselves either directly or indirectly from teachers, parents, spouses, friends, or employers highlighting their weaknesses and shortcomings. The cumulative effect of such a history can sometimes lead to internalization of these negative messages and can result in an entrenched belief that they are in fact true and unchangeable. (Nadeau, 1995, p. 135)

Terry could have sworn that this quote was taken directly from his life. He was tired and worn down from the history of his life.

Some might ask, how did Terry get into a position of needing to develop a community of one? He did have supportive family, a wife, friends, and some limited financial resources. Why didn't he just go for therapy, get on some antidepressant medication, increase his Ritalin, ask his parents for interim financial help, and so forth? Great questions. The answers lie in Terry's basic feelings of worthlessness. Finding himself in an environment in which he was so alone, with no evidence to the contrary, his feelings of worthlessness were translating deeper into self-hatred. This obstacle of self-hatred prevented Terry from considering any of the obvious solutions to his problems. It blinded him to the possibilities of help that might have been easily accessible if only he could have seen them. Terry developed a serious case of tunnel vision in which the only things he saw clearly were his own shortcomings.

Terry's feelings of worthlessness began early in his life when he went to school, began comparing himself to others, and found he didn't quite measure up. It went back to when he saw the disappointment in his parents' eyes behind their warm hugs and "good job" remarks. The teasing from peers, knowing he would always be the last one chosen for teams, and the condescending looks from certain teachers loomed before him like Times Square billboards whenever the slightest bit of evidence supported the truth of their negative assertions. At this point, Terry operated strictly on gut emotions. Time gaps, levels of maturity, and later evidence of successes all escaped his comprehension. It appeared that Terry had lost the ability to sort through distortions in his thinking. Whatever the input, his thoughts always seemed to head downhill.

Terry found himself at a place in life where he never thought he would be—initially jobless and not by his own choice, having to move cross-country for a new job that was less than satisfactory, living in an unacceptable neighborhood, embroiled in marital conflict, and having two sons who were beginning to mirror his own childhood problems. On top of all this, he was trying to deal with what Jeff VanVonderen calls a "shame-based" identity. VanVonderen states, "you suffer from low self-esteem, or a negative self-concept. You base your assessment of yourself on the 'fact' that you are a bad person, defective, inadequate, unlovable, undeserving. Even if no one else criticized you, you would call yourself a bad person" (*Tired of Trying to Measure Up,* 1989, pp. 19-20).

Of what was Terry ashamed? In his mind it started with the ADHD, a defect in how he was made. Barkley (2000), a renowned leader in the treatment of ADHD, states,

> In summary, the scientific findings from many lines of scientific research to date clearly indicate that the area in the very front part of the brain, known as the *orbital-frontal region,* and its many connections through a pathway of nerve fibers into a structure called the *caudate nucleus* (which is part of the *striatum*), which itself connects farther back into a deeper area of the brain called the *limbic system,* may be responsible for the development of ADHD. (p. 69)

Many would think, GREAT! It's not my fault! For Terry however, this was evidence that he was indeed different from other kids. These differences led to rejection, teasing, and perceived disappointment from people who mattered.

This is a key element in the experience of shame; having deficiencies, either actual or perceived, exposed before people whose opinions matter to us. Terry's shame was illegitimate because ADHD, learning disabilities, or any problem over which we have no control, are not the result of personal wrong choices. Every one of us has imperfections that are part of our life package at birth. Those imperfections do not involve an evaluation of rightness or wrongness, they merely exist and are part of who we are. Legitimate shame is the result of wrong choices that have damaged ourselves or others and need to be confessed, repented of, and corrected whenever possible.

Terry allowed his illegitimate shame, his self-hatred, and his feelings of depression to bury him in isolation. He didn't recognize, or if he did, didn't feel he deserved any resources from the community of many surrounding him. At the moment, Terry didn't even feel worthy of being in a community of one. He was operating as a robot—getting up in the morning, saying a mechanized hello to Nancy and the boys, going to work and completing tasks, coming home to eat dinner, watching TV, going to bed, and starting over again the next day. John Bradshaw, in his classic book, *Healing the Shame That Binds You* (1988), says

> Finally, when shame has been completely internalized, nothing about you is okay. You feel flawed and inferior; you have the sense of being a failure. There is no way you can share your inner self because you are an object of contempt to yourself. When you are contemptible to yourself, you are no longer in you. To feel shame is to feel seen in an exposed and diminished way. When you're an object to yourself, you turn your eyes inward, watching and scrutinizing every minute detail of behavior. This internal critical observation is excruciating. It generates a tormenting self-consciousness which Kaufman describes as, "creating a binding and paralyzing effect upon the self." This paralyzing internal monitoring causes withdrawal, passivity, and inaction. (p. 13)

There couldn't be a better description of how Terry was feeling about himself—flawed, inferior, a failure, and filled with self-contempt. Part of him knew that Nancy, Nate, and Randy were also struggling and suffering. They needed his support and strength as much as he needed theirs. However, Terry was so low, he'd have to look up to see bottom, as the saying goes. He had nothing to give to himself, much less to others. Terry knew that for the sake of basic survival, things had to change. Terry was headed for the development of a community of one.

REPERCUSSIONS OF ADHD SUCH AS JOB LOSS

When people in the United States began to have the ability to be more globally mobile, it seemed like the ultimate dream. Opportunities and life adventures would be limitless. More and more, we are realizing the huge price required for those opportunities and adventures. People now have more acquaintances than deep, life-long friendships that began in childhood. There may be little to no extended family to help with the stresses of childrearing. Long-distance moves can feel like going on a space walk and having the tether cut. A job loss on top of that feels as if you're not only drifting in space, but your oxygen is also running out. Even within the United States there are cultural differences to adjust to and different expectations regarding how people socialize and develop relationships. All of this is compounded in a negative way for people like Terry, who have personal difficulties such as ADHD, learning disabilities, developmental delays and so forth.

Without a strong community of one, it is difficult to exert the confidence necessary to enter into a strange new community of many. Terry's history of struggles centering on his ADHD contributed to his feeling like a failure. The humiliation of his job loss and his wife's disappointment in him over the whole situation kept Terry frozen. His disappointment in himself and feelings of failure kept him from even attempting to access resources that might have been helpful. He assumed that everyone he reached out to, including his wife, would instantly read the neon "loser" sign on his forehead and turn their backs. It didn't occur to Terry to check out his assumptions before accepting them as truth.

Terry's thinking became, why try? In spite of this fatalistic thinking, Terry knew the answer to the question. He genuinely loved Nancy, Nate, and Randy, and knew they were worth fighting for. Moreover, he hoped and believed that in spite of the current stressors in their lives—the fighting, the disconnectedness, and the pain—they still loved him as well.

RESPONSES TO ADHD AND JOB LOSS THAT LEAD
TO CREATING A COMMUNITY OF ONE

The key turning point for Terry in building his community of one would be recognizing that many of his expectations of success were based on past experiences, past relationships, and an environment that was now thousands of miles away. Once he realized how impossible it would be to recreate his past in his new location, he could also realize what a heavy burden he had placed upon himself. Terry had a long pattern of trying to live up to false expectations. This pattern was a burden that could weigh him down and destroy him if he did not cut it loose. As his mental clarity sharpened, Terry would be able to see the illogical nature of his thinking. His depression and discouragement, as well as his fears of failing his family, had clouded all logic. Terry knew that if this didn't change, he could lose much more than his job. His family, his mental and emotional health, and his physical health were all at stake. Terry felt alone in this battle but clearly saw that he couldn't allow that to keep him from the fight.

Terry began to realize that in creating his community of one, he needed to tackle the construction from two different sites. First, since adulthood, Terry hadn't consistently received treatment for his ADHD symptoms. He mistakenly assumed it was a kid's problem and he should be able to handle things without meds as an adult. Periodically, under the pressure of a project deadline at work, he would "give in" and take his medications. Whenever this happened, Terry would also feel that he had failed and that his personal weaknesses had won out.

He had health care insurance through his new job, so Terry decided to make an appointment with a therapist who specialized in the treatment of ADHD. He found that things had changed in the understanding and treatment of ADHD. He also recognized that the struggles he faced as an adult were different from those he had faced as a kid. "A critical goal of the therapist should be encouraging the adult with ADD to move from victimization to empowerment in relation to the ADD symptoms. The individual needs to firmly embrace the concept that ADD presents challenges which must be actively managed through a range of strategies" (Nadeau, 1995, p. 193). When he heard this notion expressed in his first therapy session, Terry knew he was on the right track.

The job loss was a second and different entity for Terry to deal with. He had never really allowed himself to grieve. The grieving was not only about the job, but also about the lost dreams he had for his future. There would be no raising the boys for their whole childhood in the same neighborhood, no growing old with people you'd met in your twenties. He had always envisioned himself as the provider and protector for his family and that vision had also evaporated. He felt he had lost status in the eyes of his wife and this was crushing to his spirit. There was nothing really wrong with Terry's life perspective, it just didn't fit reality for him at this point in time. Terry needed to find a life perspective that fit him, his personality, his circumstances, and his abilities. He needed to draw on his internal courage to question assumptions that he had always taken at face value in order to determine the truth. Terry recognized that his new life perspective needed to be based on truth in every area of his life. This became one of his primary goals as he began to create his community of one.

Chapter 6

Goals for the Real World:
Examining Expectations

APRIL'S STORY OF MENTAL ILLNESS

April sat on her bed, admiring her purchases. There were bags everywhere. She felt an unbelievable emotional high as she started sorting through the sacks. The bags were mostly filled with clothes, but she had also snuck in some matching shoes and jewelry as well. There was nothing in the world as stimulating as an after-holiday sale, unless of course, it was great sex or a good pharm party or . . . April laughed as she realized there were a number of things she could get REALLY excited about! April wished she could share all this with her mom but it was two a.m. and her mom never really appreciated her purchases anyway. In fact, her mom typically got very upset when April went shopping. She never understood how important it was for April to have a good variety of clothing and accessories so she would be ready for whatever excitement might come her way. Oh well, April would have to be excited on her own. She knew she'd be up the rest of the night. Sleep was always a stranger after sales events.

At twenty years old, April lived at home with her parents, Carl and Fran. She graduated from high school two years ago and was "kind of" in college. That meant she had flunked out her first year at the university and was now taking some make-up classes at the local community college. Only two, actually, and those were hanging by a thread. April's priority in life was to have fun and live life to the fullest! This rarely included doing homework. Every now and then, April would burn herself out and be inconsolable in her low moods. April's parents always seemed to be wringing their hands when her moods shifted. She found this very annoying and always told them she

Becoming Your Own Emotional Support System
Published by The Haworth Press, Inc., 2007. All rights reserved.
doi:10.1300/5828_06

would be fine if they would just leave her alone. When she was high, April only wanted their credit cards. During the lows, a dark room and pills would suffice. Carl and Fran often felt they were held prisoner to April's moods and April wasn't always the kindest jail keeper. There was little predictability in April's life and therefore, in family life as well.

These behavioral shifts had been going on for the past five years and several doctors later, they were still difficult to manage. The main reasons were April's lack of cooperation taking her medication, going to therapy, and participating in support groups. Truthfully, April did want help with the low moods. She would do anything to escape those times as she often became suicidal. However, April enjoyed the exhilaration of her mania, resenting and rejecting any help offered. She had genuine difficulty understanding what the problem was when she was SO happy and SO productive. She expected praise and admiration, convinced she deserved it. Instead, she got the same worried expressions along with implications that something was terribly wrong with her. It felt to April that those around her were being unloving and judgmental.

Carl and Fran were at their wits end. April had always been a difficult child. She was strong willed and had been a challenge to discipline. She had been moody, which was tough to live with at times, but they had never felt it entered into the abnormal range. It was only when her sister, Alison, came along six years after April that they began to wonder. Alison was such an easy child—easy to please, easy to soothe, and easy to discipline. At least in comparison to April. When April entered junior high school, Carl and Fran began to consider that maybe her behavior was over the top at times. Nevertheless, they continued to explain away this behavior as April being a creative kid with an exuberant personality. They just hadn't found the right niche for her. It was too frightening to think beyond that.

From Alison's birth, April had problems sharing the spotlight with her sister. There was never a time when they seemed close, as one would expect of sisters. April was always jealous and resentful of Alison. In her mind, Alison never got into trouble, was always pampered, and was definitely the favorite child. This was extremely unfair and April frequently found ways to make Alison pay for her favored status. Things would "disappear" from Alison's room, stains would appear on her favorite outfits, outrageous rumors would circulate at school from a suspicious source, and Alison's friends were frequently the target of hurtful remarks when they visited for overnights. Carl and Fran never felt comfortable leaving the girls alone for fear of what April might do. They had to be constantly vigilant in order to protect Alison from April and April from herself.

By high school, Carl and Fran began to receive regular suggestions at parent-teacher conferences that April might benefit from counseling. At first, they resisted. They believed that as responsible parents, they should be able to handle the problems themselves without having to include a stranger in the mix.

At the beginning of April's sophomore year, her parents agreed to allow her to see the school guidance counselor. They met once a week for a half-hour and after a few months, the counselor began to suspect that April's problems might be more serious than previously thought. She strongly recommended April see an adolescent psychologist to be evaluated. Fran made the appointment. Thus began a merry-go-round of treatment. April's diagnosis of bipolar illness was both a relief and a curse. They were skeptical initially yet relieved to have a name for their concerns, but felt cursed with the pain the bipolar diagnosis brought for their family. The psychologist recommended an evaluation by a psychiatrist to possibly begin medication, but Carl wanted to see if therapy alone would be effective before going the psychiatrist route. Carl wanted April to get help, but he was also afraid of how it was going to look on her medical record. He felt it might lead to having a stigma she wouldn't be able to live down. Both Carl and Fran admitted that it was hard for them to face the fact they had a daughter with a serious mental illness. They didn't want her to get labeled as crazy.

April's first major episode occurred when she was sixteen. She had been begging to date and her parents had tried to hold her back because they believed her to be too impulsive to make good decisions. She defied her parents and climbed out the window during the night. Friends from school were waiting. They felt that April's parents were much too strict, and knew that when April was in an "up" mood, she was the life of the party. And so she was. This was April's first opportunity to drink as much as she wanted and to be alone with guys. After a few beers, April's lack of inhibitions led her into a sexual encounter with Alex, a guy she barely knew from high school. She was totally unprepared for this emotionally and things got out of hand. April landed on her parents' front step at six a.m., drunk and disheveled. They were shocked and frightened to say the least.

Carl and Fran immediately took her to the hospital where April became hysterical and had to be sedated. It was determined that she had had sex, but no charges were pressed because April refused to identify Alex and no one really knew if the sex had been consensual or forced. April returned home with her family and promptly delved into her first major depression. Within a couple of months, she stopped being concerned about her appearance, quit doing any homework at all, and frequently overslept on school days. Her therapist recommended a psychiatric evaluation and by this time, Carl and Fran were willing to receive any help they could get. The psychiatrist started her on a regime of antidepressant medication. After a month or so, the medication seemed to be kicking in and April was feeling a little more upbeat. She wanted to start hanging out with her friends more and her parents felt this was a positive sign.

Unfortunately, what they did not know was that April had another sexual encounter with Alex, trying to prove to her friends that she was a real party girl. Again, it didn't turn out well and this time, April came home and took a bottle of Tylenol. Alison found her asleep with the empty bottle in her hand. April was rushed to the hospital and thus began her first psychiatric hospitalization. It became the first of many. Carl and Fran had tried to hide the extent of April's problems from friends and extended family, but now they had no choice but to let people know the truth. Besides, they needed the support themselves.

April seemed to improve and came home after a week of inpatient treatment. Everyone was hopeful, including April. She was ready for a fresh start. This lasted for a month. She did get better, *too* better. Another manic episode emerged. April stole Fran's credit card and went on a shopping spree that was the envy of her friends. Carl felt they should hold her accountable and have her pay off the debt, but realistically, April was unable to hold down a job and the debt was too great to pay off on a minimum-wage job. There was no question that April's spending behaviors put a huge financial strain on Carl and Fran.

A whole series of events began to take shape. April's life became filled with lies, stealing, sexual acting out, drinking, smoking pot, skipping school, sneaking out at night and on and on. These behaviors were interspersed with trial after trial of medications, half-hearted participation in therapy, and occasional hospitalizations after particularly self-destructive behavior. Extended family tried to be supportive, but often didn't understand the problems and were overwhelmed. Friends also tried but became tired and backed off. Carl and Fran felt they were perpetually being told to "do something," to take more control of their daughter, to try this or that. Alison was feeling neglected and cheated out of family time because of her sister's acting out. April felt alternately elated or miserable. The whole family was beginning to despair of ever having a normal life.

Even though Carl and Fran had always pitied those families who had to deal with mental illness, they had never expected to be faced with it in their own family. They felt isolated and ill equipped.

> A primary source of stress for caregivers, apart from the stress of watching their beloved child suffer from rejection by peers, school failure, severe anxiety, and even suicidality, is the unpredictability and volatility of the child's behavior when ill. Children experiencing mania or mixed states may be alternately demanding, hilariously funny, hostile, and in despair at various times during any given day. Intense and seemingly uncontrollable rages are common, and parents often must "walk on eggshells" to avoid triggering the child's fragile and hyperactive stress-response system. Families can become nearly homebound out of dread of yet another public episode. (Geller & DelBello, 2003, p. 315)

Shame, embarrassment, guilt, and fear had placed April's family in need of creating a family community of one. Even though they were severely beaten down emotionally, they were still better equipped to begin building their community of one than April. They also had life experiences prior to April when they had been an active part of a community of many. Those memories and previous experiences gave them ideas of where to start. They read everything they could find on the Internet and began seeing a therapist on their own, along with Alison. April refused to participate in family therapy at this time. In fact, April felt that her family was betraying her. She interpreted their going to therapy as an announcement to a stranger that they had a crazy daughter. Nevertheless, the others knew that whether April joined them or not, the rest of the family had to have help in order to survive.

Carl, Fran, and Alison learned how to support one another in healthy ways. They also learned how to set healthier boundaries with April and with individuals outside their immediate family. It was not always easy to set boundaries with April. She hated being contained and would do her best to find ways around their efforts. In her manic states, April considered it a challenge to escape the family's containments. It almost became a sport to her. To April's family, these games were exhausting and draining beyond belief. The family eventually discovered NAMI, the National Alliance on Mental Illness, and became active members. NAMI is a grassroots mental health organization that provides support, education, advocacy, and research for individuals with mental illness and their families.

This was fine for April's family. They had learned to access a community of many. However, April just could not connect. Internally, she felt incredibly different from everyone she knew. As her family became more emotionally healthy and cohesive, April felt more like an alien around them. She tried so hard to get them to understand where she was coming from, but the responses she received felt like rejection. She often felt foggy headed from the medications they forced her to take and when this occurred, any conversations seemed to be carried out in a long wind tunnel. Her parents and her treatment providers kept making a big deal about her substance use, and refused to try and understand her side of it. April felt that if they would all just leave her alone, she could manage her moods better with alcohol and pot than with all the medications they prescribed. She hated the weight gain, the feelings of dullness, and the affects on her sleep from the prescribed medications. Why couldn't they just trust her? She wasn't stupid!

Besides all that, April felt incredibly lonely. After several years of this, many of her friends had dropped out of the picture. They had told her she was "weird," "sick," and too unpredictable to hang around. Now in their twenties, many of them had completed college and were ready to start careers and engage in family lives of their own. They were ready to begin settling down and didn't want to risk April's sometimes wild behavior getting them in trouble and possibly arrested. April felt betrayed and began to identify more with a fringe element of people. She kept this group of friends secret from her parents. April felt that without them, there would truly be no one. There had been a couple of arrests for drunken and disorderly conduct and some of her secret behavior had come out in the open. Her parents had bailed her out, feeling that jail was not an appropriate place for someone struggling with mental illness.

Alison was now in college, studying psychology. Watching her sister go through such an agonizing existence had motivated her to want to better understand mental illness and to be better equipped to help. Alison missed her sister, or at least what she imagined it would be like to have a sister. It seemed to Alison that April was only a shadow that came and went on a breeze. She hoped that studying how to help April might also help her to feel more of a connection between them as sisters.

April only felt further alienation and anger. In her mind, Alison wanted to learn how to fix her and wanted to demonstrate that she was better than April, again in the position of the favored child. This wasn't true, but April's thinking was far more distorted than she could realize or admit.

April's parents wanted her to have an independent life as much as possible and April herself was only too happy to be on her own. She never did complete college. Typically, by the middle of each semester, she would become overwhelmed with the class requirements and either drop out or fail the course. She gave up and went through a number of minimum-wage jobs that never lasted more than a few months at a time. Finally, April began working for a temp agency and this seemed to fit her lifestyle much better. She liked the fact that the jobs were temporary and she could experience change whenever she wanted. If she were struggling with the depressed moods, she could take a few days off and still retain her employable status with the temp agency. At this point, her parents encouraged her to get her own apartment and April was thrilled. Thrilled and miserably lonely in the same breath. Another suicide attempt landed her in the hospital yet again.

Quite frankly, her family didn't have the strength to continue managing her chaotic life at home. Like many families struggling with the mental illness of one of their members, Carl, Fran, and Alison could only take so much and still survive life themselves. It didn't mean they didn't love April, nor that they didn't want to help her. It simply meant they were exhausted. They felt incredibly guilty, they worried about her constantly, but they could no longer live with April in the house. They could no longer afford to bail her out of trouble, to have things stolen, and to pay the bills from all the treatments of which she rarely took full advantage. Their dreams for their beautiful daughter had been shattered. It was highly unlikely she would be able to finish her education, get and keep a good job, or successfully marry and have a family of her own. Their expectations often had to be lowered to keeping her alive and safe while at the same time maintaining their own sanity.

APRIL'S NEED FOR A COMMUNITY OF ONE

April knew something had to change in her life or her life would be far shorter than she ever wanted. She hated having the label of being mentally ill. Although she felt abandoned by her family, she could not blame them either. She was aware of how much she had hurt them over the years. During one of her hospitalizations, she met a patient in her group therapy who challenged her to face the facts. Initially, April was angry and shocked that anyone would talk to her like that. She denied the allegations and observations of the other group members as well, but in the end, April had to admit that she was sick and needed help. She was different but it did not need to completely ruin her life. Even though she still did not like the medications, she began to wonder for the first time if that might be something she could do to help herself. She hated the thought that she might be dependent on medications for the rest of her life, but if that's what it took, maybe it was something to consider. April was finally ready to think about creating a community of one.

April's first efforts toward creating a community of one were simply directed toward listening to her treatment providers, considering their recommendations, and being more cooperative with treatment. Placing even minimal trust in people she had always thought of as enemies was one of the hardest things she had ever done. What did she have to lose? She was going nowhere fast on her own. Even her efforts at suicide had failed. She began taking her medications as prescribed. One of the first things she had to come to terms with was that the euphoria she enjoyed during her manic episodes was not normal. April had always felt that the euphoria just made her more than other people, not abnormal. This was the beginning of many things that

April had to learn to accept if she was ever going to have some semblance of an enjoyable life.

THE CHALLENGES OF REALISTICALLY LIVING WITH MENTAL ILLNESS

Both April and her family were having to face that in this situation, lowering their expectations was a necessary step to creating a community of one. Carl and Fran had to admit that the goals and dreams they had always cherished for their daughter were unlikely to come to fruition. This was especially hard for them as they saw Alison living the life they had envisioned for April as well. Realistic expectations that were actually attainable would significantly ease the stress and disappointment they felt. Even being able to live on her own, in a group home if necessary, would be a major accomplishment for April. At first, they had no idea what realistic expectations for April might look like. It was over time, through trial and error, that the whole family was able to develop expectations that seemed to be challenging and at the same time were attainable. Eventually this led to experiencing life satisfaction in a way they had missed for many years.

April and her family were, in reality, grieving. This might have been truer for April's parents as they had more of a life perspective to realize what might be lost. According to Robert Neimeyer (Doka and Davidson, 1997), "Grieving is the act of affirming or reconstructing a personal world of meaning that has been challenged by loss" (p. 170). Death is not the only thing that brings significant loss and resulting grief. Some people might argue that death, in certain instances, is easier to grieve than a chronic problem such as serious mental illness. There's an end point, a stopping place. One can move through the stages of grieving such as those suggested by Dr. Elisabeth Kübler-Ross (denial, anger, bargaining, depression, and acceptance) and be done. In April's case, as long as she lived her parents would face the reminders of great loss in their family. This didn't mean things couldn't improve or get better, but even if that occurred, they had already experienced losses that could not be recovered. Allowing herself to grieve would be a necessary part of creating a community of one for April as well as for her family.

RESPONSES TO MENTAL ILLNESS THAT LEAD
TO CREATING A COMMUNITY OF ONE

After grieving, April would need to come to terms with what she could actually accomplish and not focus on all the things she could not do or on all the things she had lost. This meant she had to live within a budget with no more spending sprees. She would have to be accountable for her money. She would have to pay her bills on time. She had to focus on stabilizing in a less stressful job. Bargains at Target or Walmart could also look fashionable if she used her creativity in a positive manner. Becoming a highly paid fashion model was just not in her future. April needed to recognize that she had many choices in managing her illness. She needed to take responsibility for those choices and learn to look ahead at possible outcomes. She had to learn that she might need other people whom she trusted to act as sounding boards for her when her thinking was confused. That required April to reach a level of humility that was initially, very uncomfortable. It took a long time for April and her family to achieve contentment with April's illness. They are not alone in this type of situation.

There are many life circumstances that drastically alter what we're able to achieve. Chronic mental or physical illnesses and disabilities require special attention to create goals, hopes, and expectations that are actually achievable. And yet, if expectations are not reasonable, frustration, bitterness, resentment, and anger often threaten to control one's life. Facing the need to accept realistic capabilities is another significant piece in creating a community of one. Although the community of many may make suggestions, only the person involved can resolve the issue in his or her heart and come to a place of peace. Imposed goals laid at the doorstep by others are rarely helpful or appreciated. In fact, goals imposed by others typically lead to feelings of resentment. When this happened to April, her response was rebellion and defiance. Maintaining a sense of self-respect and independence was more important to her than reaching others' goals.

As April began to experiment with different goals in her life, she began to develop a sense of confidence that she could determine what might work for her and bring her a sense of fulfillment. She enjoyed the challenges, solving the mysteries of how to do this or that, and even coming upon new puzzles to solve. As her confidence grew, so did her motivation to create a solid community of one. Thoughts of what it would be like to be part of a community of many became further tantalizing goals that April looked forward to achieving.

Chapter 7

Coming Out of Hiding:
Cutting the Weighty Issue
of Obesity Down to Size

LAURA'S STORY OF OBESITY

Laura looked in the mirror one last time before walking out the door to go to work. She obviously hadn't lost an ounce from the last time she peeked twenty minutes ago. She hoped the black pants and long black jacket would effectively hide the layers of fat that had crept on over the years. Truthfully, though, Laura knew that was delusional thinking. It had been effective fifty pounds ago, but no longer. Laura worked in sales, real estate to be precise. Most days now, she felt every bit as large as the houses she represented. The old saying, "he or she is as big as a barn," was no longer funny, especially considering Laura's large size and that she sold property for a living. Sales had slowly been slipping over the past few years and she had become quite adept at making up excuses. There was a housing slump, more and more competition in the real estate sales market, rising interest rates, larger down payments required, on and on and on. Although some of those things might be true, secretly Laura wondered if it wasn't because of her own appearance.

Laura was in her late thirties, never married, and lived alone. She often joked to herself that she didn't really live alone but with a twin. This was because at 295 pounds (okay, 305 pounds) she was large enough to be two people. She hadn't always been this obese, just the past ten years. Laura thought back and it still seemed like yesterday. Phil had been the love of her life. They had met during their senior year in college, finding each other during their mutual period of un-

Becoming Your Own Emotional Support System
Published by The Haworth Press, Inc., 2007. All rights reserved.
doi:10.1300/5828_07

certainty about where to go after graduation. Phil had been the practical, ambitious one with a double major in business and computers. Laura loved reading and majored in English. Phil was handsome, athletic, and charming. His only apparent flaw was a certain amount of arrogance as he tried to decide upon which major corporation to bestow his considerable personal assets. Laura couldn't wait to go along for the ride as Phil climbed the proverbial corporate ladder. He was complimentary to Laura, telling her she would be his anchor, his solid home base from which to launch his rise to financial glory.

Laura was attractive but certainly not beautiful. At that time, she only weighed 135 pounds. She now found it interesting to think that every period of her life was marked by how much she weighed. Turning the pages of a good book was Laura's favorite form of exercise. They dated regularly during their senior year and after graduation, Phil got a job at a small start-up company, thinking that if it took off, it could be his fast track to success. After almost a year of dating, and being totally smitten, Laura got a job at the local library. She was biding her time until Phil proposed and they could start their fantasy life together.

Although Laura loved being around all her favorite books, the job itself was mundane and boring. She tried to pass time with the exciting exploits of Sherlock Holmes or the bitter disappointments of Jane Eyre. Along with keeping her favorite fictional characters company, Laura began eating snack foods to pass the time. Eating out was a favorite activity she enjoyed with Phil. Of course, Phil had already clocked in a five-mile run before the meal. Laura had read about Hawkeye canoeing for twenty miles in *Last of the Mohicans*. The inevitable happened and Laura's weight began to take off rather than her career.

Phil began making small comments such as, "Why don't we forego dessert tonight?" and "Maybe you could take some of that home for your lunch tomorrow." "It looks like the dry cleaners shrunk your dress. You should get your money back on that or change cleaners." His remarks became ever more obvious and Laura began feeling very self-conscious around him. By the time she reached 150 pounds, Phil's conversations with her about weight issues became direct and pointed. "Laura, I'm just not attracted to you anymore. I can't handle the weight gain," he said. Laura tried to cut back on her eating, but now she was getting worried about the relationship. She managed her fears with comfort foods. However, her fears became reality when, at 175 pounds, Phil sent her a letter breaking off the relationship. "My future goals require having a partner whom I'm proud to show off, who will represent me well at social functions. I know this sounds shallow, but it's reality for me. I warned you and you just didn't seem to care. Good-bye."

Yes, Laura thought, *You are shallow. I never would have guessed how much. I did care and I did try, but I needed your acceptance and support. I had taken those things for granted and now I know that your love was conditional. The conditions were based on your goals, your wishes, your standards. There was no room for my struggles.* Even as Laura knew these things were true in her head, her heart was broken and her fantasy life dissolved. Phil was not her dream guy. Unfortunately, her fantasy life dissolved into cheeseburgers, fries, and cookies with extra frosting in the middle. Over the next six months, Laura hid out in the library and ate her way to 200 pounds and a solid state of depression. That was the first of many rejections that followed. In Laura's mind, all those rejections were firmly linked to her weight.

During the past ten years, Laura had come a long way. Her path was not marked in miles but in pounds. Without Phil's stellar income to look forward to, she had been forced to consider a better paying job and a real estate license seemed a quick route to a practical and potentially profitable career. There were many aspects of her job that Laura loved. She had always enjoyed decorating and many people had commented on her artsy personality. Although Laura was something of an introvert, she enjoyed working with people in small quantities. As Laura held open houses, she always had a plate of warm cookies fresh from the oven set out for potential buyers. She easily rationalized that nothing made people feel at home as much as the aroma of freshly baked cookies. She was right, but on a slow day, Laura would end up eating most of those cookies herself. She proved her point; they did help her to feel at home.

As time went on, she began to hear more comments behind her back. "I hope she doesn't knock something over. That antique vase was a gift from your grandmother and is irreplaceable. She's so big. She can hardly get through the door!" "Can you imagine having to sit next to her on an airplane?" "I'm glad we got the heavy furniture for her to sit on." Those were some of the nicer, repeatable remarks. The stares and smirks were just as potent in sending her a message. Laura's sales gradually declined and she was reminded of Phil's declarations—that appearance was an advertisement and a person had to sell himself or herself and the packaging was important.

Laura had never seriously dated anyone after Phil. His words haunted her and shaped her beliefs about how other men might relate to her. She constantly fought feelings of inferiority, depression, and despair. Laura would be the first to admit that she was desperately lonely. She was no different from many women, wanting a loving husband, delightful children, and a cozy home. These desires motivated Laura's dieting attempts. Like most people with weight problems, Laura had tried every diet on the market and was an unproclaimed nutrition expert. Nothing had worked for more than a month at a time. During her twenties, she would occasionally go on social outings with friends, hoping to meet someone who would accept all of her (literally) unconditionally. Each time it didn't happen, Laura would become more isolated and less inclined to try again. She always seemed to end these hopeful quests by drowning herself in the craving of the moment—cookie dough ice cream being a commonly recurring favorite but not the exclusive drug of choice.

Laura didn't even want to think about all the money she had spent on trying to lose weight. It could easily have been a down payment on the bright red Porsche she had always dreamed about. Laura no longer thought about that Porsche. She wouldn't have fit in the seat behind the wheel anyway. The last time she went to the doctor for a cold, she was told she was morbidly obese. Laura had never before heard such ugly words as morbidly obese. Ugly was exactly how she felt about herself. Since hitting 250 pounds about five years ago, she had withdrawn from any kind of a social life. She couldn't take any more well-meaning remarks from friends and family encouraging her to take better care of herself. As if she didn't know that! What they couldn't possibly know was how much Laura had come to hate herself. She felt like a failure—not a loser because that would have been heaven—but a total absolute failure. Why would she want to spend time, money, and energy taking care of a failure?

At that point, Laura began to think of her life in terms of all the things she couldn't do: ride comfortably in an airplane, buckle a seat belt, shop for cute clothes in trendy stores, sit in folding chairs without fear of breaking them, wear a swimsuit, slide across a booth in a restaurant without knocking the table over, walk for more than ten feet without being out of breath, sit comfortably in a compact car, sleep on her stomach, and many more. If things did not change soon, Laura knew she might lose her job, be alone forever, and never be able to do the things she had always dreamed of such as traveling, wearing short skirts and being able to cross her legs, diving into a swimming pool without splashing all the water out, etc. Many people, including her doctor, had told her they feared she might even lose her life, but that was further than Laura could think. She felt alone, defeated, depressed, and hopeless. Laura needed to turn what energy she had left to creating a community of one.

LAURA'S NEED FOR A COMMUNITY OF ONE

Laura needed to create a community of one because she felt so completely unworthy of a community of many. Not only did Laura feel deeply unworthy, but she also was deeply ashamed. A great difficulty for obese people is the unconcealable shame. It's out there for everyone to see.

> Shame generally follows a moment of exposure. It is as though something we were concealing from the world is suddenly at center stage in public view. This exposure heightens our self-awareness to a painful degree in which our entire consciousness is flooded with an awkward sense of ourselves. This heightened self-awareness is coupled with intense feelings of being inferior, defective, not good enough, fundamentally bad as a person. (McFarland & Baker-Baumann, 1990, p. 3)

This described Laura perfectly. Laura's view of herself was distorted in a very negative direction. Until she could effectively deal with that distortion in a community of one, she would always have great difficulty trying to relate to a community of many.

Her distorted thinking made it difficult to accurately perceive what others were truly thinking about her. She often turned others away because she feared their disapproval and criticism—even before they opened their mouths. Laura's motto had become, "don't take any risks where relationships are concerned." She had come to assume hurt feelings and rejection were all she could expect. Except from other fat people. However, Laura avoided them as well because that was a club of which she didn't want to be a member. A small, buried piece of Laura didn't want to give up her dream of being a healthy eater with a healthy weight. To only associate with the Big, Beautiful world seemed like completely giving up. That left her alone, needing to create a community of one.

THE STIGMA OF OBESITY

It's no wonder Laura was in such a place. In American culture, we are surrounded with weight issues. We are bombarded with advertisements for weight loss programs. Every magazine at checkout counters has stories about weight loss and the latest diet plan. Famous thin personalities on television such as Tyra Banks have done programs where they dress up in three hundred-pound fat suits for a day to see what it feels like, although she could have saved herself hours in the makeup chair and just interviewed Laura. Laura could not stand to watch the movie, *Shallow Hal* starring Gwyneth Paltrow. It was much too close to real life for her. Laura was envious and desperate to be like these beautiful people, but never seemed able to mimic their appearance in any way.

The Weight-Control Information Network, an information service of the National Institute of Diabetes and Digestive and Kidney Diseases (NIDDK), has provided data on obesity based on the 1999-2000 National Health and Nutrition Examination Survey (NHANES). According to this survey, 64.5 percent of all adults twenty years of age and older are overweight and/or obese. It is interesting to note that Sarah Leibowitz states, in a 1995 book on eating disorders and obesity, that "obesity and diabetes affect over 30 percent of our population . . ." (p. 3). How did we get from 30 percent of our population to 64.5 percent of all adults twenty years of age and older in only ten years? There is no one answer to this question. Unhealthy foods are not only readily available but can taste quite good. As a culture, we have become much more sedentary. Children sit in front of the computer rather than ride their bikes. Schedules are busy and tightly packed. The easy, convenient foods are often the calorie-laden foods. The explanations could go on and form a book themselves. However, this does illustrate a downward path in our culture regarding weight and health. It is a downward path that Laura had traveled herself. Being a part of this majority group was not the sort of "fitting in" for which Laura was hoping.

Laura knew her obesity was affecting every area of her life. David M. Garner, in a book edited by Christopher Fairburn (1995), describes this well.

> Eating-disorder patients have been described as suffering from feelings of ineffectiveness, low self-esteem, lack of autonomy, obsessiveness, interpersonal sensitivity, introversion, poor relationship skills, social anxiety, dependence, perfectionism, fears of psychobiological maturity, poor impulse control, external locus of control, conflict avoidance, developmental pathology, failure in separation-individuation, vulnerability to substance abuse, interoceptive deficits, and idiosyncratic or dysfunctional thinking patterns. (p. 119)

Could there possibly be anything left out? It's a miracle Laura was functioning at all and no wonder that isolation was becoming her primary coping mechanism.

With all of the advertisements announcing help for weight loss, why didn't Laura take advantage of them, following their direction and support, and finally take care of herself as she always should have? Laura had tried a few of these programs but found her size was not nearly as much about weight as it was about the emptiness inside of her. Nothing seemed to fill her up like a piece of chocolate chip cheesecake, but that contentment only lasted a moment before disgust and despair took its place. Although Laura was friendly, she had never made close friends easily. She never had a feeling of fitting in, of belonging. She didn't know why that was, but it was true. She had always wondered if something was terribly wrong with her and everyone else knew it but her. Was she blind to some horrible flaw that others readily saw?

Laura remembered that when she was a child her mother had made a big deal about having to buy chubby sized clothes for her. She wondered if that was the beginning of her heavy journey. Was that when she started being self-conscious about her appearance? Wondering if others were snickering behind her back because of how she looked? She clearly remembered hating those chubby size clothes that never really fit very well. One thing she knew beyond a doubt—that was when she became aware of how important appearance was to others and that she didn't measure up. Her focus shifted from the things she enjoyed such as playing and reading to wondering if she looked okay. Laura was never able to regain the focus of filling her life with meaningful things. Her focus remained outward as she struggled to please others and in the process, lost herself.

This was where Laura needed to begin creating a community of one. She realized she had no internal foundation from which to grow. Everything she depended on to gain a sense of self was external—the opinions of others and food. One reason Laura didn't want to try yet another diet program was that it would repeat the same old pattern of depending on strangers to judge if she was acceptable. There was also a great fear of failing once again. Besides, her business had suffered and she couldn't afford the programs, the special foods, and the time away from work. Laura holed up in her room one weekend to consider her situation. Extreme shame kept her away from her few friends and family. She could not stand to once again see the looks of pity or rebuke in their eyes.

Laura's story is so common that it will resonate with many. Too often, the tendency is to dwell on the problem rather than on the person who has the problem. A specific food regimen, exercise plan, and more flattering clothes will help outward appearance and affect the way we feel physically, but those things alone will not help us fill up empty places within our personhood. Jan Johnson (1993) has this to say about compulsive overeaters, "We all use food to manage the pain in our lives. That feeling of a full stomach numbs our hurt and anger. Food is our major source of comfort, celebration, and companionship. Some people eat to sustain life; we eat to face life. We eat because of what is eating us" (p. 15).

As alluded to previously, the shame that many overweight people feel is that their very size displays their inside emptiness and that they can't find personal fulfillment in a healthy way. Again, Jan Johnson (1993) describes the feeling well, "We feel like criminals who have been caught—we're exposed, tied up, and unable to move. We feel isolated, as if everyone knows our problem and feels disgusted with us" (p. 32). There has been a recent push to just accept obesity rather than discriminate against it. Plus-size models are now busy and paid well. However, it seems that this might be just another way to hide and avoid shame over an obvious problem—a trademark of obesity. It is one of those serious life problems that just can't be hidden.

RESPONSES TO OBESITY THAT LEAD
TO CREATING A COMMUNITY OF ONE

Laura needed to come out of hiding. She needed to stop hiding from her family, her friends and potential friends, and primarily, from herself. What does that mean? Creating a community of one begins with brutal honesty with oneself—to stop hiding from oneself. To do this, Laura had to ask herself some very hard questions. "What are the things I find truly meaningful in my life?" "Do I depend on others to tell me what is meaningful or can I leave others out of this?" "If food doesn't fill up my deepest needs as a human being, what does?" "Where do I find that kind of satisfying fulfillment?" "How does the way I feel about myself help me to relate genuinely with those around me?" "What does it mean to live authentically and not just attractively?" "Why have I chosen an external substance, food, to give me meaning in life?" "Why have I allowed food to become my most coveted companion, a companion who is my best friend and also a betrayer of my trust?" The answers to these questions won't be found easily or quickly, and likely not by reading how-to books. The search itself, however, is the beginning of answers.

The first brick in the road of her community of one was when Laura realized that she gave food priority over all other things in her life. She allowed food to have pre-eminence over God, her friends, her family, and herself—all the things that she always thought were most important. Laura had made food an idol that she worshipped more diligently than any faith system could have demanded. How do we discover if something is serving as an idol in our lives? We have to evaluate how much time, thought, feelings, effort, and attention go toward that person, thing, etc. What do we wake up thinking about? What do we plan our time around? What do we make excuses for? What do we cancel other commitments for? Laura was shocked when she realized she had fallen into the trap of allowing food to take the place of honor in her life. She would never have planned her life that way in a million years.

No one in a community of many could have helped Laura with this issue; it was hers alone to solve. To face the value she placed on food would cost her no money, but would take considerable time and emotional effort. If anyone else had tried to tell her what to do, it would have been Laura once again turning to an external source to find personal value in her life. Laura couldn't afford to take time off work, but every free day she had available, she spent time alone, re-evaluating the things that she wanted to honor and value. Food wasn't even close to the top of the list. However, taking care of herself was in the top ten. She came to see that her body was a gift from her Creator and deserved to be well taken care of and respected. It was quite a distortion to think that she had been pampering herself by eating her favorite unhealthy foods. In fact, she had been slowly destroying a precious gift.

The main focus of creating any community of one is challenging our thoughts, beliefs, and feelings to see if they are true. For those who struggle with body image and eating problems, such as anorexia, bulimia, or binge eating, this is no simple task. We have been saturated with many mixed messages about these issues. One commercial insinuates that cream cheese is heavenly while the next commercial tells us that thin and beautiful is the only path to being sexy and attractive. It takes extreme courage to take this on. Human beings come in all shapes, sizes, contours, and colors. We all have a mix of desireable and undesirable physical features. This is reality. To treat our bodies as precious gifts is to honestly assess those assets and liabilities. We take pride in our assets and keep them clean and polished and, depending on what they are, we either support, change, or accept our liabilities. There is also the recognition that while our bodies are valuable prizes, they are not the most important aspect of us. Our bodies are still secondary to our souls and heart.

Finding balance and perspective on this issue is a key component to creating a community of one. It is essential to have clarity about where the importance of our body fits in with the scheme of life and who we are in our humanity before we face the world and the mixed messages we will inevitably encounter. Otherwise, every new fad will leave us helplessly blowing in the wind of changes with no solid foundation. Once a mental balance is established, the next step in creating a community of one is development of a blueprint. No buildings are successfully erected without a blueprint and inordinate amounts of money are unnecessary to accomplish this task. There are mountains of resources on health and nutrition available via the Internet and the public library. Many daily television shows focus on health, exercise, and positive motivation for self-care. All are free and readily available. It is impossible to reach a goal without having a future vision of that goal. Even when we are following a recipe in a cookbook, we typically prefer to make the ones that are accompanied by a picture of the end result.

Choices must be made to implement the blueprint. Those choices are personal, solitary activities and are made one at a time. Each choice builds on the previous choice until the vision is complete. Although a community of many can provide encouragement and support, the community of many cannot make choices for us, nor can they force us to follow through. To work toward creating a vision of what one believes one should be is incredibly difficult, particularly if this vision is new, innovative, and outside the previous realm of reality. We should never fool ourselves that the choices will be easy. It took many years before the great structures of the world were made— the World Trade Center, the pyramids, the Eiffel Tower, etc. Choices are made one at a time and typically, our feelings will get in line once we're confidently headed in the right direction.

Chapter 8

Skydiving and Other Necessary Risks: Stagnant Waters Only Grow Mold

SUE'S STORY OF ALCOHOLISM

Sue pulled into the parking lot in her white Mercedes with the Bose stereo system surrounding her, playing the elegant classical music she loved. She was wearing her favorite pink cashmere sweater and black leather pants that made her look like a million bucks. Sue laughed to herself as she thought of that analogy. Her credit cards had been maxed out in order to pull off such an impression and now she couldn't even make the payments on those. Appearances were definitely deceiving. She watched as others began to get out of their cars and walk through the door in front of her. Sue thought, *This is the stupidest thing I've ever done. I don't belong here.* She pulled out her cell phone to call her friend, Claire. She was going to propose that they meet at a quaint little bar she knew, have some drinks, go to a movie, and just relax. That was all she really needed, a break from the stress. However, when she punched in Claire's number, the call wouldn't go through, and she got a tinny voice instead of Claire's informing Sue that her phone was no longer in service.

Appearances, appearances. That's all that was left. The quaint little bar down the road had been a frequent stop that just happened to be on the way to this parking lot. How ironic. The cell phone message reminded her that not only had her phone been disconnected, but that the Mercedes would be picked up tomorrow. She couldn't even afford to clean the leather pants and the cashmere sweater had a hole under the left arm. Sue's pretense that her life was wonderful was about to come to an end, whether she walked through the door or not. She began to picture herself in Wal-Mart cutoffs and t-shirts, driving around

Becoming Your Own Emotional Support System
Published by The Haworth Press, Inc., 2007. All rights reserved.
doi:10.1300/5828_08

in an old '85 Honda Civic. This was if she was lucky. Unlucky could very easily be taking a bus and checking out the latest fashions in the Salvation Army thrift store. The only part of this scenario that made her smile was imagining her mother's face as she asked her to go shopping.

At the end of the parking lot there was that door. Could it make a difference? Or would it ruin her further, if that were even possible? That door represented final exposure. It represented an end to all her charades. An end to all her pretenses. Sue had been living as if life were a mirage. It had seemed so glamorous and satisfying to anyone looking in from the outside. However, during brief moments of honesty, Sue had come to see that her mirage was only a filmy vapor. Sue was certain of only one thing. If she walked through that door, things would never be the same. Not only would other people know, but she would acknowledge to herself, once and for all, that her problems really were that bad.

Not that it mattered if *these* people knew. Look at them, standing outside that door. Smoking cigarettes in faded, worn blue jeans with holey t-shirts. Funny, they were the same outfits Sue had just imagined for herself after her downfall. These people wouldn't have a clue who Sue was, the highly successful Sue who was one of the youngest vice presidents in a very prestigious advertising firm downtown. Her anonymity was safe here; the leather and cashmere would just look out of place. Sue had done her homework over the Internet and knew that another meeting was held closer to her office—in reality her former office. It was a professional meeting, but her pride had ruled that out. There might actually be people there who knew her. Sue wasn't quite ready to give up the facade.

If she had shared the problem with her friend Claire, Claire would have recommended a fabulous spa resort in Palm Springs that also had a counselor on staff. No one would have to know. Complete anonymity. Except, Sue had to admit, Claire did know. The problem had become a little too obvious a few months ago when she had ruined Claire's party. Claire's husband had been promoted to partner status in his law firm and Claire had thrown a party to celebrate. After a few drinks, Sue had decided the lawyers were much too stodgy and stood on the dessert table and did a strip tease to loosen things up. She definitely achieved her purpose, waking up in a jail cell the next morning. Through her horrendous headache, she could hear the guards laughing about "this wild nymph who fought like a tiger" when the officers tried to help her off the table to get dressed. Why couldn't there have just been a time warp where she and the other party attendees could forget the whole episode? She knew no one would ever forget. Sue herself had very little memory except for what she was told and what she had pieced together. She had mercifully blacked out most of it.

She had tried to call Claire to apologize, but Claire had hung up on her. There was not a single friend at that party who would have anything to do with her now. She was a "social liability." Well, Claire's beautiful oak door with the leaded glass window was certainly nothing like the chipped and worn door facing her now. She wouldn't be walking in on a luxurious oriental rug with someone waiting to take her coat. According to Dr. Gerald May (1988),

> The mind tricks of addiction share yet another quality: they are contagious. No matter how much it may be kept hidden, addiction is never a completely individual thing. From the very first stages of the attachment process, other people are involved. Friends, family, coworkers, and even professional helpers affect and are affected by changes happening within the addicted person. (p. 50)

This was so true for Sue. She had always deluded herself that alcohol helped her belong socially. Indeed, she felt that she couldn't survive socially without it. There was the added delusion that others thought it funny, that they genuinely enjoyed the obscene antics that frequently resulted from a lack of inhibition. Didn't they talk and snicker for weeks after the event? At each party, didn't they encourage Sue to try and top her last performance? Well, there were no drinks inside to fortify her and no friends to encourage her this time. She didn't expect that anyone inside *this* door would be laughing about the alcohol and its effects. She wasn't feeling very funny herself now anyway. Maybe she should just turn the Mercedes around and drive to her parents' home, stay with them a while to rest, and then get a fresh start. That nice little fantasy actually helped her open the car door.

It had been a year since she had any contact with her parents, and even then, that would be all you could call it, contact. Mr. and Mrs. Friesen were among the social elite in their community. They had worked extremely hard to build and maintain an image of exclusivity.

Anyone with an invitation to a Friesen social event felt privileged indeed. Except Sue. She smiled to herself. Mr. and Mrs. "Freeze-uns" would be more descriptive. Her parents were as emotionally cold as ice. Appearances were the most important thing in the world to them. They had taught her everything she needed to know about appearances and it was now a way of life and a magnificent barrier to any genuine emotions. Nevertheless, the last time she had seen smiles on her parents' faces was when she drove into their driveway in this very new, white Mercedes that she was now sitting in. Well, those smiles would be gone once and for all after the tow truck pulled the beautiful, white Mercedes out of the driveway tomorrow.

She clearly remembered the college graduation speech she had received from her parents. "You are our only child and our hope for the future. Therefore, our expectations are high and we *know* you will *not* disappoint us. Friesens' have been an example of success and high social standards for generations in this community. That tradition *will* continue with you. We will tolerate nothing less." After her graduation gift of a trip to Europe designed to display her parents' wealth, the Friesens' fully expected Sue to begin her life of privilege and social exposure. Well, Sue couldn't get much less than she was right now and the social exposure she was about to enjoy was definitely not what her parents had in mind. The only result she could expect from walking through her parents' door was to feel it smartly hit her backside on her way out. Sue missed her parents desperately right now— at least her fantasy parents. Her fantasy parents would be right beside her, encouraging her, being supportive, telling her they loved her no matter what she had done. They would always be available whenever she needed them. Ha! With the Friesens', Sue had tried so hard to be the daughter they wanted and expected, but somehow, she never measured up.

As she sat in her beautiful car one last night, the air became suffocating, heavy with the reality of her plight. Her drinking had started out in such an innocuous way—sipping the last drops of alcohol left in elegant glasses at her parents' lavish parties. She had only been caught once, but everyone had a good laugh at the cute little girl acting tipsy and she had been escorted up to bed with no untoward consequences. Then, as a teenager, she had her own lavish parties for her friends while her parents were away on their travels. As a result, she had become one of the most popular girls in her school. Who would want to part with those credentials? In college, Sue and her friends began a game where they would visit a different bar every Friday night after classes. The goal had been to drink their way through the entire city before graduation. Sue had definitely earned an "A" on that project. There were times when she could not remember how she had returned home. More disturbing were the times she could not recognize her surroundings when she awoke on Saturday.

A couple of DUI's occurred in college, but her parents had paid the fines without question, simultaneously giving her lectures on remembering to keep her indiscretions private. After college graduation, the pressure to become successful both socially and professionally led her to become best friends with alcohol. She used it to encourage herself, to comfort herself, to numb the disappointments, and to celebrate her victories. Sitting in this parking lot before the plain, worn door, Sue had to admit that her best friend, alcohol, had betrayed her to the point of destruction. She had lost her job, her reputation, and her friends. She had filed bankruptcy and all her affluent appearances could no longer be maintained. Her health had suffered, leaving her looking haggard and old beyond her years. Sue was now completely alone, abandoned by friends, family, co-workers, and alcohol. Dr. Gerald May (1988) describes Sue's situation accurately, "The fall is tragic in the classical sense, an abject crashing down after the pinnacles of pride have been attained. Once recognized, it brings guilt, remorse, and shame in bitter proportion to the pride that preceded it. Self-respect disappears" (p. 49).

In reality, Sue had always been terrified to take risks. She was raised to fear failure and avoid it at all costs. Only alcohol had helped her gain the courage to maintain the facade of a young woman who would risk anything to get ahead. The plain, wooden door ahead of her represented the biggest risk she had ever considered, and Sue knew she had to take it on her own. Her survival as a human being depended on her courage to risk walking through the door. She picked up speed as she walked toward it, finally reaching for the doorknob, which seemed to be in the shape of a life preserver. Slowly at first, she opened the door and gingerly stepped through. Sue was definitely uncomfortable in the room of strangers, not knowing what to expect. She sat unobtrusively in the corner and listened. One by one, the strangers stood to introduce themselves and tell their stories. After a time, Sue knew they weren't really strangers at all. Every person in that room had experienced abandonment and betrayal by their best friend, alcohol, just like her.

Sue's turn came. Time stood still and Sue knew the choice of her life was now at hand. If she remained in her seat, silently bowing her head, maybe no one would notice her. Fat chance, in the getup she was wearing. Or if they did, they would hopefully take the hint that she did not want to participate and leave her alone. Sue was getting very good at being alone, but more and more, she realized how much she disliked it. She had no clue what might happen if she risked opening up to these strangers. There were many possibilities. They could stare at her saying nothing; they could ridicule her for being there; they could resent her crashing their meeting; or they might understand. Anything was possible and she just didn't know which way things might go. All she knew was that nothing was working in her life, and without change of some sort, she would have no life. They were all looking at her and quietly waiting. Sue stood up and said clearly, "Hi, my name is Sue and I'm an alcoholic." At that moment, Sue knew this risk would be worth taking. She knew it didn't really matter what the others might say or think, the risk was worth taking for herself alone. Without fully realizing what she was doing, Sue had begun to create a community of one.

SUE'S NEED FOR A COMMUNITY OF ONE

Sue needed to create a community of one because she had given her total allegiance to her best friend, alcohol. That best friend had betrayed her completely and left her clinging to life by a thread. In turn, because of her behaviors associated with alcohol Sue had greatly offended her family and social network. They no longer trusted her and certainly did not enjoy her company. Various friends and family felt they had tried to help Sue in the past, but because of her negative responses and failure to heed their advice, they had given up hope that she would ever part with the alcohol. Sue's addictive behaviors had alienated her community of many. She had embarrassed them, used them, abused them, and then left them to find others who would condone her unhealthy habits. From Sue's perspective, they no longer cared about her and their rejection had further contributed to her drinking.

This brings up another reason why Sue needed to create a community of one. Her thinking had become greatly distorted and caused her to see the world around her in a very skewed manner. She was unable to consider any other perspective than her own as having merit. Aaron T. Beck, Fred D. Wright, Cory F. Newman, and Bruce S. Liese (1993) thoroughly discuss this issue of distorted thinking and have identified seven addictive beliefs that must be corrected if treatment and recovery is to be effective.

> Addictive beliefs may be considered in terms of a cluster of ideas centering around pleasure seeking, problem solving, relief, and escape. The specific items will vary depending on the type of preferred substance. Among the dysfunctional ideas are (1) the belief that one needs the substance if one is to maintain psychological and emotional balance; (2) the expectation that the substance will improve social and intellectual functioning; (3) the expectation that one will find pleasure and excitement from using; (4) the belief that the drug will energize the individual and provide increased power; (5) the expectation that the drug will have a soothing effect; (6) the assumption that the drug will relieve boredom, anxiety, tension, and depression; and (7) the conviction that unless something is done to satisfy the craving or to neutralize the distress, it will continue indefinitely and, possibly, get worse. (p. 38)

At one time or another, Sue had fallen prey to all of these addictive beliefs and at this point in her life, it was impossible for her to think any other way.

The very nature of addictions leads one to trust the substance to meet one's needs rather than a community of many or even one's own inner strengths. In Sue's case, she grew up in a family with many dysfunctional beliefs totally apart from the beliefs associated with addictions. Thus she was already prepped to accept beliefs that are irrational and false. A major component of Sue's creating a community of one would revolve around challenging and correcting these dysfunctional beliefs. This would likely be the toughest part of her recovery, for Sue had to revamp not only her beliefs surrounding addictions, but also those surrounding family and community life. She had little idea where to begin. There had been no role modeling at home and there were no significant people in her life to reflect back to her if she were doing things correctly.

Sue also attempted to fill the empty spaces in her life by over-spending, which had led to financial disaster. She desperately tried to create an outward presentation that would effectively hide her inner distress. To a certain extent she was successful. Many of Sue's business associates had no idea of her impoverished bank account or her equally impoverished spirit. The rich and accomplished exterior had also been an attempt by Sue to gain the approval of her parents. However, the approval she sought went far deeper than, "Nice car, honey!" Sue had a hunch that her parents were as empty inside as she was, but that did not stop her from wanting more. In creating her community of one, Sue would have to learn how to fill her emptiness with a purpose and meaning greater than alcohol and unaffordable appearances. Unless a miracle occurred, she was also going to have to attempt this without genuine love and affection from her parents. Sue was going to have to risk behaving and thinking in ways that were foreign to her in order to create her community of one.

RISKS REQUIRED TO CONQUER ADDICTIONS

Why are risks so necessary? Because a new identity, one of strength, creativity, and courage, is simultaneously attractive and terrifying. Fear makes taking risks feel like skydiving without a parachute. However, risks are one more essential piece of the foundation for people who find themselves in need of a community of one. We all grow up learning scripts that tell us what to do and what roles to take. Nevertheless, there are many people, due to various circumstances, who reach a place where the script ends, such as Sue. The writers of the script are nowhere to be found, and the individual finds himself or herself utterly alone, struggling to write a second or third act and not knowing the ending. The only roles Sue was taught to play ended with very bad reviews from the critics.

Old scripts become comfortable habits, even if they are no longer working effectively. Risk-taking challenges those comfortable habits. Risks may expose the dysfunction of old patterns or highlight that things have changed, and not the way one might have chosen. Risks may expose our vulnerability, especially when there is no support system to act as a net. However, to avoid risk-taking in a healthy way is to stay stuck in a life pattern that may lead to hopelessness, depression, and utter loneliness. For Sue to stay stuck in her alcoholism would eventually mean complete self-destruction. Avoiding healthy risk-taking may mean the loss of our self-respect, allowing fear to rule our lives. Taking risks is necessary to propel us on a forward path. One can look at risks fearfully and take them through clinched teeth or one can see them as a great adventure filled with surprise, wonder, and awe.

RESPONSES TO ADDICTIONS THAT LEAD TO CREATING A COMMUNITY OF ONE

In order to take that first risk or even consider it, one must be willing to treat oneself with kindness. With all of the self-recrimination that often accompanies alcoholism or any other addiction, this will likely be incredibly difficult. Treating oneself with kindness when taking risks is essential because of all the uncertainty involved. Initially, there may be no clear idea of how to go about taking the risk or where it might lead. The very nature of risk is that the outcome might have negative and unpleasant consequences as well as significant gain. Everything is in the realm of the unknown. We could fail, maybe again and again. Without kindness and understanding for self, those failures could end in self-destruction. What does this kindness look like? It certainly involves a lot of positive self-talk. "I know I looked clumsy, foolish, or awkward, but it's my first time and with practice, I will get better." "Learning how to live without alcohol, food, gambling and so forth is a whole new way of life. I need to allow myself time to gain new knowledge. I certainly didn't learn algebra in a day." "If others criticize my lack of skill as I try this new thing, maybe it's because of their own fears. I don't need to take it personally." "It's been a tough fight to stay sober today. I deserve a warm bath with a good book. The dirty dishes can wait until tomorrow." Most of us would treat others with such kindness in a heartbeat. There is no reason we should not do it for ourselves.

Kindness also includes the notion of grace. The standard definition of grace is receiving something good that we know we don't deserve. It may be true that we've made poor choices for a long time. These poor choices have been harmful to ourselves and very possibly to those around us. We may have freely chosen to spend the family's resources on alcohol, food, shopping, or gambling. Others may have had to go without necessities in order for us to indulge ourselves in our addictions. We may feel we deserve the misery we experience as the result of our negative behavior. To stay in that misery may feel like well deserved self-punishment. Guilt can be the seal that keeps us tight in that position of misery.

Grace is coming to the understanding that even though I may deserve painful consequences for the damage I've caused to myself and/or others, I can take the risk to pursue recovery. I can give myself permission to want my life to get better. Grace is saying to ourselves that forgiveness for our past negative behaviors is possible. It is saying that I am worth the pleasure of living life sober, the pleasure of enjoying a positive bank account, and the pleasure of enjoying healthy relationships in spite of what I have done. Yes, I may very well need to make amends and others may or may not respond positively to my efforts, but I can make those amends and I can do my best to repair broken relationships. Kindness and grace for ourselves propels us forward, motivating us to implement the necessary risks for progress. Kindness and grace for ourselves are necessary components in creating a community of one.

Chapter 9

A Leap of Faith: Exploring
Strange New Worlds

DIANA'S STORY OF DOMESTIC VIOLENCE

"Mrs. Brown, what happened to your face?" This innocent question came from the mouth of Brittany, one of the children in Diana Brown's kindergarten class. "Did you fall off your bike and bump your head on the sidewalk? That's happened to me before. It really hurts!"

Diana knew before she left for work that she would have to come up with some logical explanation for the kaleidoscope of colors around her left eye. Actually, she had a whole catalogue of excuses ready at her fingertips. The trick was picking one she hadn't used in awhile. This wasn't the first time she had gone to work with a black eye, and if Matt continued on this course, it was unlikely to be the last time.

"Brittany, how did you know? I was out rollerblading last night and tripped over a tree root." Diana could hardly believe how glibly these things rolled off her tongue.

"Wow, Mrs. Brown, you rollerblade? That's so cool! You need to wear a helmet though."

The caring nature of the children she worked with brought tears to Diana's eyes. It was the main reason she loved her job and loved coming to work. Diana's home life with her husband, Matt, felt so barren in comparison to this wonderful group of kindergarteners who were so full of life and love. The kids kept her sane and Diana frequently pretended that this classroom was her real home. These were the children she could never have with Matt. There were times when it was very difficult not to cross her professional boundaries and just grab

Becoming Your Own Emotional Support System
Published by The Haworth Press, Inc., 2007. All rights reserved.
doi:10.1300/5828_09

them all up, smothering them with hugs and draining them of the affection she craved. She wanted to give them homemade cookies with milk, plan their birthday parties, and be there on Christmas morning when they came to see what was under the tree. These were all the things she had always dreamed about and things that had been denied to her by Matt.

Around lunchtime, the school secretary, Alice, knocked on Diana's classroom door and entered the room with an ear-to-ear grin. In her hands, she was carrying the most beautiful bouquet of peach roses Diana had ever seen. "You must have the most amazing husband in the world, Diana. We in the office are absolutely overflowing with jealousy!" gushed Alice.

"Yes, he is quite amazing." Diana was more amazed at how adept she had become in lying and covering her tracks. "I was telling the kids how I clumsily fell over a tree root rollerblading last night. Matt felt terrible that he didn't reach me in time to prevent the fall. I guess I should start learning a new sport."

The roses were indeed glorious. The attached note just said, "Sorry, Love Matt." Diana wondered how long the sorry would last this time. Better yet, why couldn't the sorry Matt be the husband to whom she was married?

As the day went on, Diana's side began hurting. During her break, she had noticed a huge bruise had formed around her left rib cage. She hoped it wasn't another cracked rib. She had made so many trips to the doctor with suspicious injuries during her marriage to Matt that she now avoided it whenever possible. It was better to just wrap it when she got home and hope it would heal on its own. Goodness knows she kept all the first-aid supplies on the market at home. Three o'clock was fast approaching and she needed to begin focusing on how to enter the door at home. After one of these episodes, re-entry was critical. The way she approached Matt that first evening back together would determine whether they moved on as normal or whether the episode would be repeated and expanded. Early in the marriage, she had responded with anger and demanded that he apologize, make amends, get help and so forth. It had all backfired. She quickly realized how much stronger he was than her. Fighting back was extremely dangerous. The humble wife who apologized for her clumsiness and who made his favorite dinner was the one who stayed safe for at least a few months.

Diana hated herself for going the safe route. She would be the first to admit that her marriage had cost her every ounce of self-respect. Diana knew she deserved better, but after ten years of marriage to Matt, she didn't know how to get it. Without her teaching job where she was constantly surrounded by children who adored her, Diana knew she just couldn't go on. Prior to their marriage, Matt had never said anything about not wanting children. Diana had just assumed that children were part of the marriage package. It turned out to be a very wrong assumption. After the wedding, Matt had made it very clear that he didn't want to share Diana with anyone, including children. At first, Diana was somewhat flattered that she mattered so much to Matt. However, she learned the hard way that she was very naive.

During their third year of marriage, Diana "accidentally" became pregnant. She believed Matt to be similar to many men who thought they didn't want children, and then when the little one arrived, he would go bonkers. She also believed that having a baby in the house might soften his angry and aggressive moods. She was very wrong. Diana was twelve weeks into the pregnancy before she got up the nerve to tell Matt. She wanted to make sure before sharing such good news. Matt just stared at her in disbelief. "Why, you conniving little bitch! If you think you can get away with defying me, think again." Matt insisted on an abortion and Diana refused. If there was anything that she would stand up to Matt for, it was this blessed baby within her. The baby felt like a lifeline. She tried in every way to convince Matt that the baby would actually enhance their marriage, joining them together even closer than before. He didn't buy it.

As mean as he could be, Diana never expected the push down the stairs. The stair spindles flew past her vision until finally she saw nothing but darkness. She awoke in the hospital overhearing Matt telling the doctor in a choked voice that she had lost her balance carrying a basket of laundry down the stairs. He had tried to reach her, but he wasn't quick enough. She was still semi-conscious as Matt told the doctor how much they had hoped and planned for this baby. If he had been carrying the laundry for her, this would never have happened. He would never forgive himself for the loss of this child. How would he ever be able to tell Diana that she would never be able to have more children? The damage was irreparable. As Diana saw the doctor consoling Matt, she felt her own truth would never be believed and she was trapped.

Matt was a model husband for at least three months, then he informed her it was time to get over it. The look in his eyes changed from caring concern to a hardness that Diana knew from past experience. He meant business and Diana stopped grieving.

Family and friends encouraged Matt and Diana to be positive and to think of adopting after some recovery time. Diana longed to share with her family the true grief in her heart, but there was never an opportunity. Matt made sure of that. Either he went with her to visit family or she didn't go at all. What did Diana hear? How lucky she was to have such an attentive husband! So few men these days would stand up for their wives like Matt did. Most men would gladly dump their wives off and go play cards or golf with their friends. It went on ad nauseum. Diana came up with the line that their hearts had been set on having children of their own and adopting just wouldn't be the same. Then Diana buried herself in her teaching and the subject was never raised again. Little Brittany had no idea what her admonition to Mrs. Brown to wear her helmet really meant.

The cycle continued for several years—the quiet Matt filled with underlying tension, the rage filled Matt who exploded in violence, and the remorseful Matt who showered Diana with apologies and gifts. Diana's own cycle consisted of only two stages—fear and more fear. After seven years, Diana felt she couldn't take anymore. Matt controlled the finances so she had hidden away some household monies until she had enough saved to consult an attorney. She had concluded that Matt was not going to change and she wanted a divorce.

Diana was surprised that the attorney believed her story of hidden violence in the home. He suggested she get a restraining order as the first step to freeing herself from Matt. He also gave her advice about paperwork she would need to gather in order to proceed and a list of expenses which included his fees. Diana was completely overwhelmed. Matt controlled everything. She had no money of her own and no access to any of the joint money. She was clueless about where he might have important paperwork stored. She couldn't even make an appointment with the attorney in the open; she developed a severe headache during a school day in order to come.

Diana desperately wanted to talk with her parents about her situation but was terrified to do so. Matt had warned her more than once that there would be serious consequences if she said anything to anyone. He threatened that even her family would not escape his wrath, in fact, the repercussions for them might be even worse. Remembering a broken wrist, a few broken ribs, and more than a few black eyes, Diana believed him without question. After speaking with her attorney, Diana decided to try a logical and rational approach. It seemed reasonable that Matt must be as unhappy as she was. How could anyone enjoy being angry as often as Matt? Maybe if she presented the subject of divorce as something in his best interest, he would see that things could be better if they were apart. She would ask for no support, let him have the house and the assets, and all she would ask for would be her freedom.

One evening when Matt seemed to be in a good mood, she asked if they could talk. Sensing nothing out of the ordinary, Matt agreed. Diana probably wanted an increase in her clothing allowance. He was in a good mood, and feeling generous, decided in advance that an extra fifty dollars a month wouldn't break him. Diana tentatively began to ask if Matt were happy. She commented that he seemed to be angry a lot and thought that maybe their relationship was the cause. Maybe she just wasn't the right wife to make him happy. Matt looked down and said nothing, and Diana continued. She remarked that although she cared about him deeply, maybe it would be better for him if they went their separate ways. She told him she wouldn't fight a divorce if that would free him to find someone more suitable.

That night, Diana came within inches of losing her life. Without a doubt, it was the worst beating of their ten-year marriage. Matt took her to the emergency room and told the attendants that she had been mugged while walking in the neighborhood. They were skeptical, but Diana went along with the story. The police were called and asked for a description of her attacker. Diana, now an expert in the art of fabricating a quick story, told the police that the attacker had come from behind and had knocked her unconscious before she saw anything about him. Matt worriedly sat by her bedside and emotionally implored the police to find the person responsible. He wanted this madman behind bars experiencing the full extent of the law. Diana remained in the hospital for a week. Her hospital room was flooded with flowers from Matt, but the best part of the experience was knowing that for at least a week, she would not have to worry about being beaten again.

If nothing else, this last experience made Diana fully aware of how fragile her situation was. There was no more denying that her life was in constant danger as long as she remained with Matt. Although Diana knew better than to ever mention separation or divorce again, in her secret thoughts she began to wonder how she might gain her freedom. For the next three years, Diana did whatever she had to do in order to survive. During that three years, Diana began to save little bits of money here and there—from the grocery allowance, doing her own hair and saying she went to the beauty shop, buying clothes on sale and saying she paid full price, going without lunch at school, anything she could think of. She also began doing some research on the school computer during lunchtime. She looked up anything she could find on domestic violence. It was slow going, as she had to be careful not to be caught. Diana asked Matt for a gym membership for her thirtieth birthday, laughingly saying how she was now going to have to work harder to stay in shape for him. She then hid extra money, paperwork she was gathering, and other information in her gym locker. Diana was in the beginning stages of creating a community of one.

DIANA'S NEED FOR A COMMUNITY OF ONE

Diana found herself in need of creating a community of one for a multitude of reasons. Like many wives, Diana had been raised to believe that her marriage vows were sacred, not to be broken for *any* reason, including an abusive spouse. Furthermore, Diana came to believe that if Matt was abusive, it was her responsibility to figure out how to placate him. After the last beating, when she came so close to being killed, this notion began to shift.

Roberts and Roberts (2005) discuss why some women become chronic victims. They assert that there are four concepts that may contribute to women staying in abusive relationships. The first is traumatic bonding. "Traumatic bonding is a strong emotional attachment that can develop, combined with fear of abandonment and intermittent abuse." The second concept is intermittent reinforcement which "occurs when the abusive partner is periodically kind, loving, and apologetic for past violent episodes, promising that the violence will never happen again, but then resorts to degrading insults and abuse." The third concept, learned helplessness, "refers to a victim who learns from repeated, unpleasant, and painful experiences that she is unable to control the aversive environment or escape; as a result, she gradually loses the motivation to change the abusive situation." Finally, "Minimization describes a victim's distorted cognitive beliefs when she grossly underestimates both the frequency and severity of the battering incidents she has endured" (p. 18).

All of these concepts related to Diana at one time or another. Early on in the marriage, she had indeed minimized Matt's abusive behavior. Matt grew up in an alcoholic home where he witnessed domestic violence between his parents. His drinking father controlled the family with an iron fist, and Matt determined that no one would ever control him like that again. Knowing all this about Matt's family, Diana had tried to be understanding at first. She felt that he just didn't know what a healthy marriage could be like. Diana didn't have much more knowledge of a healthy marriage than Matt. Her own parents had divorced when she was five years old, but the bond between them was maintained with blaming and arguing. The verbal abuse that flowed between her parents left Diana clueless about healthy communication and assertiveness.

In the early years of the marriage, Diana was afraid that Matt would leave her. With her belief that marriage should last forever, she was very fearful of what others would think of her if her marriage failed. She determined that her life would be very different from that of her parents'. For many years, she was taken in by Matt's sincere sounding apologies and the wonderful make-up gifts. Then as time went on and the abuse worsened, learned helplessness entered the picture. After consulting with the attorney, presenting her desire for divorce, and subsequently being beaten almost to death, Diana felt helpless. And yet, there was a small spark of defiance deep within her that was willing her to fight for her life. That small spark was encouraging her to begin creating her community of one. In Diana's case, that community of one might be a literal one as well as figurative in nature. Out of fear she distanced herself from family and friends. Out of fear she allowed Matt to take control of all her material resources. Diana knew that if she were to have any kind of life worth living, it would have to begin within her own being, a community of one.

Another significant piece of Diana's experience that led her to need a community of one was the complex array of loss she endured as a victim of domestic violence. The multiple losses Diana felt led her to loneliness in which, for all practical purposes, she and her abuser were the only two people in the world. Carol Adams (1994) expresses this quite well.

> First, she has lost safety—and the normalcy and peace of mind that accompanies one's sense of safety. Second, she has also lost the ability to set boundaries and have them and her privacy respected. Third, she may lose her sense of reality as it is displaced by the abuser's sense of reality, her sense of direction as the abuser's control overwhelms it, her sense of decency and her belief in decency as it gives way to violation and being violable. Fourth, she begins to lose or loses her self-esteem, ability to trust, confidence in herself, sense that the world is just and that God is just. Fifth, she feels an increasing sense of isolation from others and may experience a diminishment of interpersonal resources. Finally, concepts and feelings such as faith, hope, charity, worth, innocence, goodness, joy, love, connectedness, intimacy, and purity are all seriously undermined. (p. 17)

Wow! What a list! Is it any wonder that Diana waited ten years to begin creating her community of one? The wonder is that she began to think in this way at all.

DARING TO TAKE A LEAP OF FAITH

The most vivid picture of a leap of faith occurred in *Indiana Jones and the Last Crusade* starring Harrison Ford and Sean Connery. Indiana Jones went through several trials in order to reach the Holy Grail and save his mortally wounded father. The last trial was the leap of faith. He came out of a tunnel that abruptly ended with a perpendicular precipice. Across a giant chasm with no bottom in sight, he could clearly see the Holy Grail that would save his father's life. His instructions were simply to take a leap of faith. This leap of faith appeared to end in certain death. Indiana had a choice to make—believe that the instructions were valid and would lead him to the Holy Grail or leap to certain death. Choosing to take the leap of faith, an optical illusion became a visible bridge as he stepped out, enabling him to safely cross over the chasm and reach his goal.

Diana's leap of faith, like that of Indiana Jones, seemed as if it would end in certain death. Matt had threatened her life many times if she even thought of leaving him. He came close to succeeding a couple of times when leaving wasn't even the issue. However, Diana came to believe that if she didn't take the leap of faith, her internal death was just as certain. She concluded that she would rather die with a sense of self-respect due to her own choosing and not due to the unpredictable will of Matt. Diana was in her early thirties and had no desire for any kind of death. Therefore, in thinking about making changes in her situation, she was initially flooded with terror. Like Indiana Jones, she had to step out. She had to begin to believe in herself. She had to have faith that there were better things for her across that seemingly bottomless chasm in front of her.

RESPONSES TO DOMESTIC VIOLENCE THAT LEAD TO CREATING A COMMUNITY OF ONE

Matt had purposely removed any resources that he thought might give Diana the ability to challenge his total control. From Matt's perspective, it was all about control. It is unlikely that Matt would have labeled it as such, but nevertheless, control was the name of his game. It had nothing to do with Diana, his marriage, his public image, or his manhood. Diana learned about this too, through her reading on the Internet at school. Once she understood what the real issue was, control, she had a much better idea of what she was up against in regaining her freedom.

Diana's first decision concerning her violent marriage to Matt was whether she would remain a victim or move on to creating her community of one. Victims feel they have absolutely no choices available to them. They are at the mercy of another individual whom they believe to be more powerful than they are in some way. There were many issues in Diana's life that had pressured her to remain in a victim role. First, Diana had been desensitized to verbal and emotional abuse by having observed the destructive relationship between her parents. Destructive relationships were her norm. It was a small step for her to become desensitized to physical abuse as well. Second, she felt she was genuinely in love with Matt when they married. After watching her parents' divorce, she had determined she never wanted that to happen to her. She had believed for a long time that if they both worked hard at the marriage, they could overcome the problems.

Knowing Matt's background, Diana felt sorry for him and had felt that with love and kindness she could help him heal.

Third, Diana was an educated, intelligent woman who was very successful in her teaching career. She was extremely ashamed and felt guilty about what was happening in her life. Even though she often minimized the abusive treatment she received, there was also that smart, accomplished professional side of her that knew no woman should have to put up with that kind of treatment. The fact that she did put up with it was an embarrassment she had difficulty overcoming. Diana was also ashamed of all the lying and deception she had engaged in to try and keep Matt's reputation from being tarnished. She reasoned that when he realized how badly he was treating her and began working hard to change their marriage for the better, she didn't want him to have to deal with the negative opinions of people who knew the truth. What a blessed fantasy! She now realized that the only thing she had accomplished with lies was to isolate herself from people who might have been supportive of her.

A fourth issue that had kept her in a victim role was her own self-doubt. Diana sometimes couldn't help but wonder if there were things she was doing to cause Matt to resort to violence as a way of relating to her. Had she missed some terrible flaw within herself that was really at the root of the problems? Matt certainly intimated that often enough. What if he were right? If there was even a fraction of truth in the terrible accusations that Matt made against her, maybe she deserved to have some sense knocked into her. Certainly not to the extent that Matt had done, but why couldn't she get it if something was that wrong with her? How could she leave Matt and maybe have another relationship in the future if she were such a flawed individual? Diana was an honest person at heart, and if there were deficits in her that needed fixing, she really wanted to know.

Diana's finances, or lack thereof, also pressured her to remain in the victim role. From the beginning of the marriage, Matt had insisted that he handle all the money. Diana had been very impressed with this at first. How many men these days were so responsible? She didn't question his demands that she turn over all her paychecks to him. He had told her it was just easier for one person to be in charge and that, of course, all their assets were mutual. It had sounded logical to Diana and Matt had always given her a reasonable amount of money to manage the household. So, ten years later, Diana found herself in a position where she was clueless what her financial obligations were with Matt. She also had no way of accessing money that she had legitimately earned through years of hard work. She was having to sneak money, a little here and a little there, just to get legal consultation.

All these issues pressured Diana to form a victim role for herself. In creating a community of one, Diana renounced the victim role by facing the truth of each obstacle. She found the strength to believe that she did have choices in her life. She also realized that by making choices, she actually was putting herself in a dangerous position. Although she didn't want to believe that Matt would take her life, she knew she couldn't trust him when he was in a rage. And there was no mistake that Diana's making choices for herself would precipitate a rage. By taking on the responsibility to make choices and begin creating a community of one, Diana also had to protect herself. Matt had already approved her gym membership, so she didn't have to worry about signing up for self-defense classes. A police officer taught the classes and she was able to discreetly ask his advice about how to physically care for herself.

Trust, or the lack of trust, was another huge barrier for Diana to overcome in creating her community of one. She was quite aware of the fact that she could not deal with this mess alone. However, she had been isolated from family and friends now for years. She had many acquaintances through her teaching position and her gym membership, but absolutely *no one* knew Diana's real world. Because she had kept all these people at a very long arm's length, Diana didn't know whom she might trust to help her. One wrong move and she could end up dead. She also had no desire to put anyone else in danger. Diana decided the place to begin was with people who had experience in dealing with domestic violence. She easily found the National Domestic Violence Hotline number: 1-800-799-SAFE (7233). Calling that number would be the first step.

Pride was the next barrier. Even though she knew she needed help and knew she couldn't break free alone, she still struggled with the thought of other people knowing. What would they say? Would they wonder why she had waited so long to get help? Or, why would a professional woman put up with such debasing treatment from her own husband? Diana broke through those objections in her head, but then the woman on the other end of the hotline number immediately suggested she needed to come to a shelter to be safe while they helped her figure things out. A shelter! With who knew what kind of women! A college graduate, a teacher who had worked hard to achieve a successful position in life—in a shelter! Diana slammed down the phone. It was a slap in the face that got her attention more than any hitting Matt had ever done. In a million years, Diana could never have imagined herself in a shelter, sharing personal space with other strange women whom she didn't know anything about. Only that they shared a common horror—a loved one had betrayed them and their lives were in danger. If she allowed it, pride could slam the door and seal it tight against any creation of a community of one.

Diana needed to face all of this to reclaim herself and be capable of becoming part of a community of many. She would have to immediately renounce her victim role and learn how to recognize, create, and follow through on choices. She would have to learn how to prepare and endure the consequences of those choices. The positive choices might very well be as difficult to experience as the painful ones. Nevertheless, the freedom to make choices, even the freedom to experience the consequences of those choices, was an integral part of her humanness. It was a part that she had relinquished for far too long. Diana would also have to face the truth of her life. Since childhood, she had created a fantasy world in order to survive. She remembered all the stories from her own childhood that she had shared with her kindergartners. Stories of loving parents, playing with the neighborhood gang, and having not a care in the world. The stories continued into high school with the wonderful support she felt from her parents as she left for college. All of these stories neglected the truth that she would have done almost anything to get away from home.

Then there was the truth about Matt. She would have to face the fact that dating had not been the fairy tale she had always told. The only stars in her eyes had appeared after Matt had slapped her a couple of times and the main romance occurred as he tried to get her to forget the stars. The most frightening part of facing the truth was that Diana didn't know if she would recognize it or if she could hold onto it as a course to live by. She always felt that survival was not possible without fabrications, embellishments, and yes, lies. For Diana, truth had always been a very dangerous commodity.

Facing the truth revealed loss. Tremendous loss. It came from every aspect of her life. She lost her fantasy memories, her wonderful fantasy marriage, her self-respect, her financial security, and her very identity. Diana felt she would drown with the grief. She had felt sorry about things before, but her own self-defenses had prevented her from ever before experiencing authentic grief. Now it was unavoidable. It took all the courage she could scrape up not to hide from the grief. In spite of the pain that she would have desperately liked to avoid, she instinctively knew that there were things she must learn as a result of this suffering. She always tried to teach this lesson to the children in her classes in a small way. "I know you don't like sitting in time-out and missing recess, but you will learn from this that you must not hit Sally when you get angry." Now that lesson was coming home to her; suffering had a purpose in large ways as well as small.

Even if she had had a wonderful support system, with loving, caring people standing in line to help her, this leap of faith had to be Diana's alone. Facing the truth, grieving, learning through suffering, and making choices were all things that had to be taken care of in a place of aloneness. Diana was about to be reborn into a strange new world. The world Diana thought she was living in was really only an illusion. The nice home, handsome husband, great job, and smiling faces were a facade for intense pain and suffering. Now it was time to move on to a world of authenticity—real fears, real loves, real grief, real joys, and real growth. This is what it means to create a community of one. It grows not out of loneliness, but out of aloneness. To stay in a place of loneliness is to refuse to learn from the pain. It can make a man or woman dependent on anyone who might offer relief. It is a place of vulnerability and can be a set up for further pain and suffering. Aloneness is a place of strength. It is a place where individuals like Diana can discover their own identity apart from the dictates of others and a place where their inner strengths can become foundations for taking them into a community of many. Aloneness is the birthplace of a community of one.

SECTION II:
BARRIERS TO CREATING
A COMMUNITY OF ONE

Chapter 10

Taking the World by Storm:
Facing Our Fears and Moving On

Fear is one of our most powerful emotions. Giving in to fear can keep us in a quagmire of misery and overcoming it can lead us on to "taking the world by storm." But why is it so powerful? One reason is that fear causes us to distort, deny, or avoid the truth. Truth is one of our highest ideals and is often very demanding. Knowing the truth may require us to take action that is terrifying. When Dan discovered that his most respected spiritual leader was dishonest, that truth required examining his own spiritual beliefs, exposing the dishonesty, and publicly going in a different direction. For Dan, this became a lonely journey leading him to become a community of one. Denying that truth would have meant Dan was collaborating with the dishonesty. He likely would have felt miserable inside and most certainly would have lost self-respect.

Without a doubt, this ongoing battle between truth and lies is one of the many obstacles to creating a community of one. Buying into false beliefs about ourselves can lead to loneliness, fear, and a defeated life. Where do these false beliefs come from? Often they come from others with whom we have close relationships, such as blood relatives or long-time friends, but who have hidden agendas or outright opposing goals and values. For example, take Sue and her parents. They adamantly believed that social success was the ultimate value and pressured Sue to accept that belief as her own. For years, Sue was afraid to challenge that belief. She was afraid of tearing apart a parent-child bond that was never really in place. Alcohol became Sue's ally in maintaining her fears and denying the truth.

Because of the close ties to these people, we may be blinded to their hidden agendas or fearful of challenging their values. Some-

Becoming Your Own Emotional Support System
Published by The Haworth Press, Inc., 2007. All rights reserved.
doi:10.1300/5828_10

times the appearance of having a close connection seems important to maintain in spite of the fact that there is no closeness. No one enjoys being part of a major family quarrel or scandal. Illusions of relatedness, whether to family or friends, may seem better than nothing at all. However, these fears pressure us into accepting falsehoods as a basis for relationships. These fears keep us from allowing the illusions to evaporate. Maggie's fears of finding out that her marriage to Jake was a sham led her to prefer a superficial connection rather than risk sharing authentic emotions. Only relationships based on truth will bring about genuine satisfaction and enjoyment and successfully lead us to be confident members of a community of many.

A second reason fear is so powerful is that it can paralyze us, keeping us immobile in the midst of difficult circumstances. This was certainly true for Diana. Her life was legitimately in danger and she felt a position of paralysis in response to her fears was the only way to survive. We can allow our fear to convince us that to move forward or to try and change our circumstances in any way would be disastrous. Maryanne knew that Tom was far less than the wonderful husband and father she bragged about to others. However, her fears that others would think poorly of her and that she couldn't manage as a single parent kept her imprisoned in the marriage. The worst fear of all was wondering if Tom was right, if she really was the inadequate idiot he kept scorning. Maryanne's fears led her to the dark despair of depression and isolation, leaving her in need of a community of one.

Fear is an emotion that encourages us to resist change, even though cognitively we may know without a doubt that change is necessary. Fear deceives us into believing that we are inadequate or incapable of making the necessary changes. Fear convinces us that change will only make things worse, that in reality, there is no hope for improvement in our situation. Fear tells us to stay where we're at, where we're comfortable with the chaos, where at least we know what to expect. Fear tricks us into accepting the lie that change will bring only failure and personal destruction. Fear reminds us of times in the past when we've tried to change and things didn't work out. Fear doesn't allow us to think through the difference between impulsive, poorly planned changes and those that are researched, well thought-out, and implemented with care. Fear kept Terry back in elementary school, listening to the taunts of peers and the unfair reprimands of his teachers.

His fears convinced him that his belief of being unable to do anything correctly, was in fact, true.

The greatest obstacle to anyone becoming a supportive member of a community of one is fear. If fear cannot be faced and overcome in a community of one, we will not be able to move forward to become one in a community of many. There will always be individuals in a community of many who will readily use our fears against us for their own gain and personal agendas. Some might say that fear can also be a healthy emotion. For example, shouldn't we be afraid of stepping on a rattlesnake in the desert? Or, shouldn't we be afraid of getting assaulted when walking alone at night in a neighborhood with a high-crime rate? The answer to those types of questions is "Yes, of course." However, that type of fear is more related to having respect for the potential consequences of being in a dangerous situation. That type of fear leads us to cautionary behaviors, recognizing the risks, and preparing to manage those risks in the safest way possible. That type of fear encourages us to take action to maintain our well-being. It doesn't imprison us, or paralyze us, or diminish our self-esteem.

Fears are frequently based on assumptions. Those assumptions may have little or no evidence to support them. Fear-based assumptions often project negative consequences into the future as if those were the only possible outcomes. They deny the equally likely possibility that the future might hold good and enjoyable outcomes. Fear-based assumptions are frequently magnified by our own creative imaginations. Our imaginations can easily string one unlikely negative outcome to another and another, leading to an end result that would even be daunting for Superman. Assuming shadows are real, the monster in the closet is not just a bad dream, and the end of the world really is going to occur next week are assumptions without supporting evidence. They are impossible to manage and overcome rationally—necessary steps to move forward with healthy productivity.

How do we face those fears that say, "You're nothing in light of these overwhelming circumstances. So just give up and give in"? Laura could easily decide that losing 150 pounds is an impossible task. She could allow her fears of ridicule to keep her from going to the gym. Her ingrained fears of rejection because of her weight could keep her from ever achieving the life of her dreams.

Facing our fears is especially difficult when we find ourselves in situations that leave us in a community of one. Theoretically, we would want a partner to lean on, to provide us with support and encouragement. Wouldn't it be nice to have a whole group of people saying, "What can we do to help?" In a community of one, those thoughts may be fantasies. People who find themselves in a community of one have come to a crossroads. They must decide if they will stay unhappily in their current situation or if they will choose to face their fears. This is an unavoidable encounter for those who want to move forward with their lives. April needed to decide if she would continually go through the revolving door of the psychiatric hospital ward, or if she would face her fears of medications and other treatments to create her community of one.

Facing our fears begins in our minds. We must come to the place where we say, "No more! No more living my life on the basis of fear! No more living my life as a prisoner of fear! No more allowing fear to control my every thought and action!" These thoughts themselves will likely be accompanied by fear, but there is a determination to proceed in spite of that fear. The choice must be made for fear to no longer be allowed to be an overwhelming obstacle, no longer be allowed to be a controlling force which shapes the future. In other words, fear can no longer be allowed to be in the driver's seat. It's time to pull off the freeway into the rest area, take a break, and change drivers. This is how we choose freedom. Freedom is a mental choice that doesn't involve circumstances.

Once this decision has been made, the tide has turned. We will begin to get stronger. A starting point in facing our fears is asking questions. Is this fear realistic? Is there any evidence to suggest that the fear has some legitimacy? If so, what precautions should I take? Is this fear out of proportion to the situation? Is this fear being encouraged by others who might not want me to be more independent for some agenda of their own? Have I used this fear as an excuse to not take risks? Is this fear based on old experiences that are no longer relevant? What are the possible outcomes of putting this fear aside and proceeding? How has this fear kept me stifled? How has it prevented my personal growth? Will discarding this fear cost me anything? If so, is it worth it? How will I feel about myself if I hang on to the fear? Thoughtful analysis of our fears will help to prepare us for future action.

Fear may start with an element of reality such as forgetting your lines in an elementary school play. Maybe a few of your peers even laughed at you. Unchecked, this fear can become magnified to unbelievable proportions. People can come to believe they can never again speak in public without evoking laughter and humiliation. Over the space of years, fear such as this can become so huge a person may experience agoraphobia, a fear of any social contact outside their own home. Unchallenged fears can become monsters. We must confront our fears early on. Initially, we may have to do the hard work of slaying monsters of fear. As we develop our supportive community of one, we must make a solid agreement with ourselves that we will not allow our fears to grow to such proportions in the future. Monsters can be tamed.

Another very important thing to consider is whether we want our lives to be based on fear or truth. Fear can lead to what we call cognitive distortions. On the other hand, cognitive distortions can lead to irrational fears. What are cognitive distortions? They are thoughts that go through our minds that have elements of truth in them, but not the whole truth. Cognitive distortions are thoughts that are half-true, partially true, or even minimally true. The rest of the thought is false in some way. It may be an out-and-out lie or a slight twisting of the truth, but in some way, it negates the total validity of the thought in question. Unfortunately, the piece of truth which is present in the cognitive distortion is often very powerful and makes it hard to let go of the pieces that are false. The true part has likely been reinforced in a significant way at some point in our past history. We buy into the true part and then generalize that the whole thought is true.

How does this play out? Take this for example. Maybe in junior high school Terry took a risk and joined the school choir. He was very excited to have been given a small solo to sing at a performance. As often happens with boys entering puberty, his voice cracked. Unfortunately for Terry, it cracked in the middle of his solo. All Terry heard after that was laughter—not the applause, nor the appreciation for the rest of his performance. Terry developed the cognitive distortion that he was incapable of singing. He held onto this thought even into adulthood. Terry already had a fairly lengthy history of having feelings of inadequacy reinforced. When others would hear him singing quietly in a group and comment on the nice quality of his voice, he would become embarrassed, never able to accept the compliments.

Even though Terry loved music and singing, he eventually quit out of the fear of being laughed at. If Terry had challenged that cognitive distortion, he would have realized that his voice cracking was due to a normal physiological process that is temporary in nature. Although he may not have had the talent to become a professional singer, Terry would likely have been able to sing very successfully in choir, at special events, or even in a band with friends for his own enjoyment. That one embarrassing occurrence, added to previously reinforced moments of shame, generalized to a lifetime of believing he couldn't carry a tune.

In creating a community of one, cognitive distortions have to be challenged and corrected. If we have the cognitive belief that no matter how hard we work at a new job we will still fail and be humiliated, we will never gather the courage to try. Our fears will keep us from doing a job search, submitting applications, and going on job interviews. However, if we examine that belief and search for the truth, we might discover that it is only true on occasion. If a teacher decides to apply for a construction job and has no prior building experience, the fear of failure might be a reality even though he or she works hard. A teacher's job skills are more related to writing and instructing than driving a nail. A teacher who searches for a job related to his or her prior training will be basing his or her life on the truth of their abilities. If April adamantly insisted on pursuing her dream of becoming a high-fashion model, her fear of not succeeding might have been supported in light of the bipolar illness that gave her special challenges to overcome. The intense stress of such a career would have seriously jeopardized her mental health.

Sometimes our fears are warranted. If a person has bullied us at school, at work, or socially for years, the issue must be addressed. Some people engender fear in others and then use that fear as a weapon of control. It is an extremely effective weapon and hard to neutralize, but continuing to avoid the fight solves nothing. A person victimized by fear must examine that fear intelligently: Where does it come from? What is its hold? What will defeat it? Fear is more an enemy than any human being could be; a victim must make it clear that fear will no longer be effective. Many aggressive individuals who use fear to manipulate others will back away once they've observed the tactic no longer works. There is no more jubilant feeling than to recognize freedom from fear.

Bullies often have many fears themselves and have chosen to manage their fears through aggression. What do bullies have to be afraid of? They are often afraid of their own perceived inadequacies, their potential failures, and their internal emptiness. They might reason that if they attack those who trigger or remind them of these fears, they can keep the fears at bay and maintain the facade of control they long for.

Freedom from fear is synonymous with safety. Perhaps not physical safety, but more important, emotional safety, psychological safety, and spiritual safety. How can this be? Because when we're no longer worried about what other people will say, do, or think about us, we are safe in the places of our being that matter. Yes, of course our physical safety is never fully guaranteed and physical death awaits all of us at some point. Why do we care so much what other people will say, do, or think about us? It's because we are created to be social beings. There is nothing more pleasurable or satisfying in life than to be part of a close and loving relationship with another human being. Our faces beam when our efforts are praised by someone who matters. We experience comfort and relief when a respected friend empathizes with our struggles. At the same time, we cringe in dread over the criticism and derogatory remarks of an unkind person. Some people never recover from that type of wound.

To be fearless is to be at peace in our souls. Brennan Manning (2000) describes it as being at home:

> Home is that sacred place—external or internal—where we don't have to be afraid; where we are confident of hospitality and love. In our society we have many homeless people sleeping not only on the streets, in shelters or in welfare hotels, but vagabonds who are in flight, who never come home to themselves. They seek a safe place through alcohol or drugs, or security in success, competence, friends, pleasure, notoriety, knowledge, or even a little religion. They have become strangers to themselves, people who have an address but are never at home, who never hear the voice of love or experience the freedom of God's children. (p. 143)

In creating a community of one that is free from fear we are creating our own safe home.

Chapter 11

Guilt Must Go!: Guilt Can Be Good But Needs to Be Temporary

We might readily agree that guilt must go. It's a most unpleasant feeling and can often cost us dearly in the sleep department. Is it craziness to say it can be a good thing? I don't think so. Similar to other emotions, guilt has a very positive purpose. The purpose of guilt is to make us aware of wrongdoing and the resultant problems in relationships. Because it is such an unpleasant feeling, guilt is also a strong motivator. Unfortunately, many of us are self-centered enough that we wouldn't always take care of unpleasant business such as correcting wrongs we've done if we weren't motivated to feel better—in other words to say good-bye to guilt. Becca Cowan Johnson (1996), also points out that guilt can be both a fact and a feeling. She states,

> *Guilt* is what we should experience when we do something wrong. It is a behavior-correcting device. *Guilt feelings* are what we experience when we think we've done something wrong. That is, we may experience guilt feelings both when we have and when we haven't done anything wrong. (p. 27)

Sometimes we feel guilty when we actually haven't done anything wrong. It's only a perception, or maybe it has been insinuated by others that we *should* feel guilty about something. There are also instances in which the basis for our guilty feelings changes. For example, there was a time when girls were told they should feel guilty if their skirts were short enough to show ankle. Or boys were told it was wrong and therefore worthy of guilt, if their hair touched their shirt collars. Women who dressed like men with pants and shirts would go to hell for sure!

Becoming Your Own Emotional Support System
Published by The Haworth Press, Inc., 2007. All rights reserved.
doi:10.1300/5828_11

Obviously, those grounds for guilt are long gone. New rules have taken their place. Legitimate guilt would be much easier to spot if there were specific rules about right and wrong that never changed; if awareness of those rules was obvious to all; and if everyone agreed with the validity of those rules. That's much too easy and simply not the case. Many times the only way to determine if guilt is legitimate is our consciences. Can we live with ourselves over whatever it is that we have done?

Unresolved guilt can be a real trickster. Left to its own devices it can play with our minds in a very negative manner. It can be very diligent in trying to convince us that we are unworthy of moving forward, of having positive things in our lives, even of having good feelings about ourselves. It may try to tell us we deserve the pain we're experiencing. Unresolved guilt can even lead us to believe that any suffering we might experience as a result of actual or perceived wrongdoing is completely justified. When you consider that society, often on a regular basis, changes the standards of what constitutes wrongdoing, you can see how easy it is to be taken in by guilt as the trickster. The danger here is the temptation to subdue our conscience, in order to rid ourselves of the discomfort of guilt. A sensitive conscience that challenges us to consider and evaluate our guilt is an ally that we should highly value.

When dealing with guilt as a barrier against creating a community of one, we're not concerned with the fickle rules of society, but with guilt that stems from genuine wrongs we have committed. Is there any such thing as a never changing standard of right and wrong? I believe there is. Murder, theft, lying, cheating, and so forth are going to be wrong no matter the society or the point in history. A general principle of determining legitimate wrongdoing is the question, "Have I harmed another human being in some way, either physically, emotionally, cognitively, or spiritually?" Is it wrong for me to have a glass of wine for dinner? In most cases, the answer would be no if the wine would not physically harm me. However, if I were to have a glass of wine in front of Sue, who just went to her first AA meeting because her life had been decimated by alcohol, it would be very damaging and might cause serious damage to our relationship. What if I plan a birthday party at the beach for Joan? Who could argue with that? Isn't that being a very thoughtful friend, probably going to a lot of expense to honor my friend Joan with a birthday celebration? The hot sun at the beach could easily precipitate a lupus flare for Joan. To choose a beach party to celebrate Joan's birthday would be insensitive at best.

What if I invited Laura to go shopping with me for spring clothes? Let's pretend that I have an ideal body shape that shows most clothing styles to the best advantage. Maybe I'm trying on new spring shorts and a halter top and prancing around in front of the mirror, remarking to Laura how great the outfit looks on me. Is there anything wrong with that? No. I'm just having fun. However, if Laura is severely shamed over her obesity, self-conscious in front of other customers whom she imagines are snickering about what *she* would look like in the same outfit—my actions would be insensitive to say the least. Although not wrong in itself, my behavior would be incorrect because it inflicted emotional damage on my friend Laura and again, would likely create significant distance in our friendship.

Most acts of genuine wrongdoing damage relationships. For individuals who have a strong spiritual faith, acts of wrongdoing will also damage their relationship with God. In the examples of Sue, Joan, and Laura, my seeing the hurt looks on their faces would hopefully inspire me to feel a sense of guilt, which would motivate me into taking action to repair the relationship. That brings us to the next step in dealing with guilt. What do we do about it? I believe there are three things that need to happen in order to effectively deal with the emotion of true guilt, the kind of guilt activated by genuine wrongdoing.

The first is to own our wrongdoing and confess it, initially to God and then to the person(s) we have offended. Second, we need to make amends if possible. There are some things that can't be replaced or fixed—the person offended may have died or moved to an unknown location. We may contact that person and find that they refuse to see us. A broken item may be a one-of-a-kind heirloom and irreplaceable. In such instances, we will need to be creative and do the best we are able to mend fences. At the very least, we can offer our most sincere apology for our behaviors. Finally, when the previous two steps have been completed, we need to let go of the guilt. It has served its purpose and needs to move on. A significant part of letting go of guilt is the acceptance of forgiveness. Hopefully, the person we've offended will be forgiving after our confession and amends. If not, we must forgive ourselves and not allow the incident to prevent us from moving forward in a positive direction.

Some very positive results occur from handling guilt in this manner. Although we have no control over how the other person(s) involved will respond to our attempts at making amends, hopefully the relationship will be improved. Certainly, our relationship with God will be enhanced. When the other individual(s) witness the courage needed to apologize and see our efforts to repair damage, the relationship may well become stronger and tighter than ever. When people share experiences that involve depth of character, the bond between them also takes on greater depth. If we carelessly spill a glass of wine on someone's new carpet, glibly say sorry, and begin discussing the day's weather, that relationship will remain superficial if it lasts at all. Appropriately dealing with our guilt will bring about a clear conscience. The value of having a clear conscience is inestimable in terms of mental health alone. A clear conscience frequently leads to unaffected self-confidence, a tremendous asset to those who want to create a community of one.

Our self-esteem and sense of self-worth are also enhanced when we handle our guilt in a positive way. It takes a spirit of humility and courage to openly admit we've done something wrong, that we've harmed another person, and that we're not perfect. A healthy pride arises when we've faced these difficult and unpleasant emotions and done the right thing. All of this releases us; it frees us to continue on our path of personal growth. Guilt can become an internal cancer that weakens and prevents healthy growth. When guilt is removed through our actions, our strength is restored. We are typically energized and eager to move forward. Through this process of acknowledging our wrongdoing and dealing with our guilt we gain knowledge. We learn how to better interact with others in ways that are more careful and respectful of their boundaries and feelings. We gain knowledge of how God works in our lives and leads us down a better path. At this point, guilt has served its purpose and no longer has a positive purpose in our lives.

Unfortunately, many people hang onto guilt beyond its positive intent. Thus the wall that might easily prevent someone from creating a community of one begins to grow. One reason people hang onto guilt beyond what is appropriate or helpful is because they feel they deserve to be punished. They believe that the wrong they committed was so heinous that they deserve the misery of incessant guilt. This is an act of self-condemnation and is never helpful. It denies that we feel guilt for a productive reason—recognition that we've done something wrong and need to take care of the damage we've caused. Self-condemnation keeps us downtrodden and actually prevents us from righting wrongs. It also sets us up as our own judge and jury. We reach our own verdict of guilty and we impose a sentence of "you can never do enough to fix this." This conclusion may be a serious distortion of the truth.

Many people hang onto guilt out of fear. They recognize the legitimacy of their guilty feelings and may want to deal with those feelings, but fear blocks their way. These individuals may be afraid of how the offended party will respond: Will they criticize me? Scream at me? Disown me? Ridicule me? Embarrass me? They might wonder if their guilty confession will make things worse. Some situations may get worse before they get better. A fearful person may not be able to see through the worse to the better, so they just avoid the situation and feed their fears instead. This results in the worst occurring and the better never arriving. Some may be fearful of what amends might be required of them. Amends can be very costly, both personally and financially. Amends may be achieved only at great sacrifice. What is it worth to have improved relationships and a clear conscience? What is it worth to have a cleared path for future growth?

Some individuals may hang onto guilt out of denial. It may be too painful to acknowledge personal deficits and they hang onto a certain amount of guilt rather than admit the extent of the damage they've caused. A friend of Terry's might say, "You are so scatterbrained all the time! Why can't you just settle down and focus?" Terry's response to such an unkind remark might be silence and withdrawal with a hurt look on his face. Although his friend might notice this and feel bad to a certain extent, he minimizes the damage by saying, "Oh, I didn't mean anything by it. I was just teasing. You're being too sensitive." This denies the damage to Terry's emotional well-being, but the friend would rather feel mild discomfort from guilt than admit the depth of his hurtful comment to Terry and give a meaningful apology.

Some people hang onto guilt because of the attention it brings them. To be in such misery because of guilt over something, to be uncertain of what to do about it, to be besieged with fears, and to have one's life in constant turmoil because of such a situation can be used to evoke great sympathy from others. Even though people may easily and quickly tire of giving that type of attention, the person receiving it may have a moment of enjoyment that he or she is reluctant to give up. The guilty person can take on a martyr role that is not valid in the true sense of the word, but can be milked to appear very noble for the purpose of getting sympathy and attention.

There are also individuals who hang onto guilt out of pride. They may readily admit they wronged another person and even feel guilty about committing the offense, but they will not be the first to approach the party they offended. They might say, "Well, if you only knew what *they* did, you would understand why they should be the first to make this right," or "They threw the first insult, so I had every right to respond in a like manner. I refuse to apologize until they apologize first." These individuals fail to recognize that hanging onto guilt out of pride and stubbornness will bring them and whomever else is involved ill effects.

This is closely related to hanging onto guilt out of sheer rebelliousness. Tom might have said to Maryanne, "I don't care if I did have an affair, I refuse to apologize. You had it coming because you were acting so stupid! You brought it on yourself." Someone like Tom deals with guilt by numbing feelings, and may eventually eliminate them altogether. This is true of individuals who develop antisocial personality disorder. One characteristic is the absence of conscience when wronging another person. It is a dangerous state of affairs for that person and potentially can lead to a complete inability to emotionally relate to others. A more dire result is that a dulled conscience can lead to a life of crime.

Many negative side effects are incurred from hanging onto guilt beyond its legitimate purpose. These negative side effects directly inhibit the creation of a community of one. The first negative side effect is the distance created in relationships, both with other people and with God. When we have wronged another person in some way and have refused to deal with the resulting guilt, it hangs between us and the other person like a dark cloud waiting to explode at any time. We are very uncomfortable any time we're around that person or maybe even when we're around other people close to that person. We might begin to imagine that others know more about our guilty offense than they actually do. Where that relationship is concerned, we may begin a process of withdrawal and avoidance. Our failure to approach the person(s) we've offended may become an offense in and of itself, compounding the original damage done. The ultimate side effect of retaining our guilt may be the dissolution of the relationship altogether.

Our sense of self-esteem and self-worth will likely suffer when we hang onto guilt. For those whose conscience is still healthily intact, guilt is a constant reminder that we need to *do* something—confess, apologize, make recompense, and so forth. When we continually avoid dealing with our guilt, we don't feel very good about ourselves. If the person we've offended is close to us, we may be constantly aware of the pain we've caused. Disappointment in ourselves may lead to self-doubt, self-recrimination, and eventually self-hatred if it goes on too long. Again, healthy guilt has a purpose, and that purpose is for our well-being, not our detriment.

Stifling our conscience may seem the only way to rid ourselves of unwanted and unpleasant guilt. Even if a person has decided not to deal with the guilt, it's still there and accusing that person of his or her wrong. Some individuals would rather dull their conscience than deal with the guilt. This is not only a negative side effect of retaining guilt, it's a dangerous one. Once the conscience becomes dulled, it becomes easy to continue harming others, and the degree of harm may increase and intensify. Guilt and conscience serve as restraining forces on our hurtful behaviors. They serve the important purpose of helping to keep society somewhat civil. Our prisons are overflowing with individuals who dealt with guilt by dulling their consciences. Once it is snuffed out, it is very difficult, some would say impossible, to retrain a person to have a conscience.

There are very real physical side effects associated with hanging onto guilt. Headaches, abdominal upset such as vomiting, constipation or diarrhea, tension in the muscles, sleeplessness, loss or increase in appetite, the development of depression, and loss of energy can all result from unresolved guilt. This is primarily due to the stress and anxiety which unresolved guilt can generate. Depression and anxiety disorders may also develop if unresolved guilt persists. The anxiety of feeling always on guard in case the guilt is discovered is a very unpleasant way to live. Over an extended period of time, it may even be difficult to remember the original issue of guilt. A person might easily begin focusing on the physical issues and begin a chronic round of problems and treatments, when properly managing the guilt would have prevented it all. In this case, people can choose to spend their time and money on medical treatment or on making the amends necessary in the first place. This is a strange position to understand, but certainly happens many times.

Inappropriate guilt may also masquerade as being spiritual on many levels. Johnson (1996) addresses this issue and states,

> When overcome with guilt we may condemn ourselves and incorrectly assume that God is also condemning us. We may deny ourselves pleasure or possessions as a means of atonement. We may seek to cleanse ourselves from our sins through a frenzy of Christian service. Or we may begin to avoid God or turn from our faith because of the burden of our guilt. All of these attempts at running from guilt serve only to alienate us from the One who is able to heal and help us. (p. 100)

Failure to properly deal with guilt on a spiritual plane can lead to feelings of unworthiness regarding a spiritual connection to God or motivate a person to continuously pursue forgiveness and redemption.

We may feel that our guilt makes us more spiritual and more worthy of God's notice. This is distorted thinking, but the rationale is that the guilt reminds us of our place of humility before an all-powerful God. It may fool us into believing that false pride over our self-righteousness has been eliminated. Either perspective—paying unnecessary penance or spiritual elevation—completely denies the truth of God's mercy and forgiveness when we take responsibility for our guilt, confess it, and make amends to the best of our ability. This is explained in I John 1:9 (NIV): "If we confess our sins, he is faithful and just and will forgive us our sins and purify us from all unrighteousness."

The ultimate repercussion from hanging onto unresolved guilt is the prevention of further personal growth. I would venture to say that healthy forward motion on any personal level is impossible if unresolved guilt is present. The creation of a community of one cannot occur until guilt is addressed and resolved. Guilt will continue to be a barrier if one tries to access a community of many; making genuine, authentic connections with others will be difficult to impossible. What does one do to remove this barrier? The first step is to ask, "Have I actually done something wrong?" "Is this a true judgment of myself and what I'm feeling?" "Is this residual guilt I'm hanging onto even though I've already taken care of my offense?" "Is this guilt being imposed on me by others for their own purposes?" Johnson

(1996) suggests that "We must test, check and evaluate our guilt feelings before we accept them as accurate, reliable indicators of guilt" (p. 130).

When we begin to ask ourselves these questions, we must also determine what standards we use to evaluate the answers. If we are using the opinions of others, changing social standards, customs that may vary from place to place, or the dictates imposed on us by others, we may not be evaluating our guilt accurately. For example, some individuals use guilt as a manipulative tool to impose control on others. If Maggie had refused to go golfing with her father and Uncle Ed because she knew she would likely experience abuse, but her father told her she should feel terrible for embarrassing him in front of Uncle Ed, should she feel guilty? No. This is not legitimate guilt. Maggie's father is trying to control her with guilt for his own negative purposes. Maggie was simply trying to protect herself.

Guilt can also be used as a weapon. Sue's parents, for example, might have said to Sue, "How dare you go to that Alcoholics Anonymous meeting in that sleazy neighborhood, openly associating with people who are such an embarrassment to society? I hope you feel guilty for shaming us in such a way!" Should Sue feel guilty? No, not for going to an AA meeting. Perhaps during the course of her alcoholism, Sue lied to her parents about her alcohol use, or stole from them to get money for alcohol. These offenses likely hurt her parents emotionally as well as financially. That is legitimate guilt and Sue will need to confess and make amends in order to exorcise her guilt in a healthy way. However, to feel guilty because she doesn't accede to her parents' determination of what type and class of people are proper to associate with is not legitimate guilt. More people would likely applaud Sue's actions than be shamed by them.

Once it has been determined that the guilt is legitimate and deserving of attention, then one needs to work through the healthy steps of acknowledgement of wrongdoing, confession to God and others involved, making amends where possible, and then saying good-bye to the guilt. For those prone to guilty feelings or insecurity in their ability to determine legitimate guilt, it may be helpful to write down what happened, the steps that were taken to deal with the guilt, and the outcome and the date it all took place. Then if guilty feelings return over the same event, one can decide if it truly was unfinished or if these feelings just need to be evaluated in a different manner. Guilt can hang on beyond what is helpful and healthy. If guilt has been dealt with but the feelings continue to return, one must ask if there is something else behind them such as the desire for self-punishment. If this is the case, then it's no longer the guilty feelings that need to be addressed, but the perceived need for self-punishment.

Self-evaluation is a main tenet in creating a community of one. Assessing guilt that may be a barrier to moving forward requires honest self-evaluation that may be very difficult for someone who has felt the burden of guilt for a long time. It may seem presumptuous to even question whether the guilt is legitimate or not. That in itself may be a huge step forward. This is an issue that may feel too overwhelming to tackle alone. One simply may not trust his or her own judgment in the matter. It could be helpful to talk about this with a close, trusted friend. Or if that feels too threatening, to access a resource that is required to keep strict confidences such as a priest, pastor, or rabbi. If one has the resources, this might be an excellent reason to consult with a therapist.

Sometimes guilt may be related to breaking the law and a person might be very hesitant to discuss the matter with anyone. If it comes down to it, that individual will have to determine whether possible physical imprisonment is worse than the prison of a guilty conscience. Their guilt may have led them to fear consequences which might not even be realistic. There are also people who might forego pressing legal charges if appropriate amends are made. There are no guarantees, but the point is, guilty people may assume things are worse than they might actually turn out to be. Fear of consequences does not excuse a person from having to face his or her guilt. Guilt has no place in the creation of a community of one and much less in a community of many.

Chapter 12

Corralling Crazy Thinking: Correcting Thought Distortions

The mind is, without a doubt, the most amazing and most complex creation in the entire universe. Even after many years of study, I continue to find the workings of the brain completely overwhelming. Our brains are involved in how we process information, how we feel about things, how we direct our behavior, and how we interpret experiences. It is utterly essential as a tool in creating a community of one. Richard Lazarus remarks (Freeman, Simon, Beutler, & Arkowitz, 1989), "Cognition is the key to functioning and change; it provides motivational direction, emotional significance, and the justification of action, and it connects action to the environmental context by the principle of feedback" (p. 99). He says that as important as cognition is in the process of change, it is not sufficient on its own. Motivation and emotions must be congruent with cognition for healthy change to occur.

Many times the loneliness and isolation we experience during difficult circumstances either stems from distorted thinking or is influenced by it. This makes a great deal of sense. If the truth about our situation in some way threatens or saddens us, it is a very effective defensive technique to distort that truth. It is amazing how easily we can convince ourselves that no one will help us, that there is no one who cares, and that no one would ever enjoy our company. There may not be a shred of evidence for this except our own distorted thinking. We can put a new slipcover on an old couch and get rave reviews about the new décor. It's still an old couch underneath. Thus, we also see the contribution of emotions on our thinking. As human beings, we have the capacity to twist the truth in many creative ways to make it more palatable. Sometimes we do this consciously and other times it is beyond our conscious awareness.

Becoming Your Own Emotional Support System
Published by The Haworth Press, Inc., 2007. All rights reserved.
doi:10.1300/5828_12

Many would agree that what goes into our minds largely determines the type of person we are and can influence the direction of our future behaviors. This is a sobering thought when we consider all the negativity with which we are bombarded in our society. Much of it we simply cannot avoid. This sets the stage for a grand battle. A significant component of creating a community of one is clearing our thoughts of negative material and correcting any thoughts that do not stand up to the light of truth. Although there might be many understandings of what the meaning of truth is, the truth referred to here is about those beliefs and life principles that have proven unerringly correct over time. There are facts in history that people believed to be true but with the discovery of new knowledge are now known to be false. Examples include the world being flat, the sun being the center of the universe, smoking being a harmless pleasure, and so forth. Authentic truth is that set of facts, beliefs, values, and principles that do not waver with the introduction of new knowledge, new fads, new ideas, or new opinions.

This battle for our minds begins in childhood. In her book, *Consuming Kids* (2004), Dr. Susan Linn discusses the targeting of children by the media.

> Today's children are assaulted by advertising everywhere—at home, in school, on sports fields, in playgrounds, and on the street. They spend almost forty hours a week engaged with the media—radio, television, movies, magazines, the Internet— most of which are commercially driven. The average child sees about 40,000 commercials a year on television alone. (p. 5)

Dr. Linn talks about the exposure of children at a very young age to escalating scenes of graphic violence and sexually explicit material. These issues, together with the promotion of rampant materialism, prompted Dr. Linn to say, "Parents have cause for alarm. People who highly value material goods (an orientation reinforced by consumer marketing) are likely to be more unhappy and have a lower quality of life than those who value more internal or nonmaterial rewards such as creativity, competence, and contributing to the community" (p. 8). I believe that in time, the notion that children and adolescents can be exposed to sexual material, violence, drugs and alcohol along with other examples of clearly adult behaviors yet not be harmed in some way will prove to be false.

Putting these types of thoughts into our minds from an early age can set the stage for needing to create a community of one, and can set us up for a serious struggle in effectively creating that community of one. Because our minds are such marvelous creations and work phenomenally, we seldom completely forget images and thoughts that gain access to our brains. This behooves us to be extremely careful of the types of thoughts, sounds, and pictures that find their way into our minds. Many will have problems with this notion of screening our input. There is a great deal of controversy in our society today about what constitutes free speech and artistic expression. Many will advocate broadening our horizons by exposure to a large range of material, with both positive and negative implications. However, for those who find themselves in need of a community of one, those who have struggled with obsessive and distorted thoughts, with impure mental images, with disturbing sounds, and with fearful memories, the freedom of exposure to so much disturbing material is not a freedom that's welcomed or productive.

Many of the so-called cognitive or thought distortions that we struggle with are a direct result of needing to protect our minds and memories from disturbing and frightening images. Maggie was quite accomplished at this skill of self-protection. When her father would inappropriately come to her bed at night to snuggle, Maggie distorted that memory to one of her father taking the time to show her special affection and comfort. Aaron Beck is a well-known pioneer in the field of cognitive psychology. He describes cognitive distortions as a return to a primitive information-processing system in which there are systematic errors in reasoning as a response to psychological distress (Freeman et al., 1989). Beck identifies six types of cognitive distortions.

The first is called *arbitrary inference*. This involves coming to a certain conclusion in spite of a lack of evidence to support that conclusion or even when confronted with contradictory evidence. For many years, Maggie wanted to believe that her father was a wonderful man who thoroughly enjoyed the company of his little girl. She arbitrarily believed that her father was a good, kind man because that's what fathers should be and that's what she wanted to believe her father was like. The contradictory evidence that Maggie chose to ignore was the fact that her father enabled Uncle Ed to sexually use his daughter.

The second type is called *selective abstraction* and occurs when a situation is conceptualized based on a detail taken out of context; all other relevant information is ignored. April easily fell into this type of thinking. She could have done a very creative collage in occupational therapy, received praise for it, and the next week believe she could have a fabulous career in graphic art. All this in spite of the fact that her bipolar disorder caused her moods to be so erratic that it was hard for her to complete a single class in college. April selectively focused on her success with one art project and ignored the detail that she was failing in school.

Next is *overgeneralization,* which happens when a few isolated incidents are used to formulate a generalized rule. Laura experienced this after hearing some cruel teasing about her weight from a couple of kids in high school and generalized that as an obese person, she would never be able to make friends easily. In actuality, she had a very pleasant personality that would have drawn many people to her for friendship if she had allowed it to be seen. She developed a whole belief system about the friendliness of people based on the negative behaviors of a few of her peers in high school.

The fourth type of cognitive distortion is *magnification and minimization.* This distortion occurs when a situation is given much greater or much less credence than it actually merits. Terry may have experienced this distortion in his job. His ADHD made it difficult for him to focus, otherwise he might have noticed his boss' frustration over his lack of organization on the job. Terry minimized remarks in his annual evaluations that stated he needed coaching in organizing his work. He ignored the need to develop organizational skills that might have improved his chances of keeping his job. On the other hand, Maryanne magnified Tom's criticisms of her personality and capabilities to the point that she was fearful of ever experiencing any personal success without his help.

Personalization is another type of cognitive distortion and it involves the attribution of external events to oneself. Dan frequently blamed himself for the difficulties in his church. He often felt that if he were more assertive, his children wouldn't have experienced so much distress at school. Or, if he had been more creative with business ideas or trusted the pastor more, he wouldn't have experienced the ostracism of his fellow parishioners. By taking all the blame on himself for the problems he and his children experienced in their church and school, Dan failed to hold the people accountable who actually were responsible for the insensitivity, dishonesty, and harshness.

Finally, there is *dichotomous thinking*. This happens when an experience is described in extremes (Freeman et al., 1989). Joan often fell into this trap in dealing with her chronic illness. During her flares, she would lapse into thinking that things would never get better, that she would never be able to engage in productive work or go out with her friends or experience long walks in the woods. In reality, her flares were intermittent and during remissions, she was quite capable of all these things. April easily fell into this trap as well. In her manic episodes, a shopping bonanza where she maxed out all her credit cards was just taking advantage of a few sales for things she needed. In her depressive episodes, April felt that life wasn't worth living even though she had many things going for her such as a loving and supportive family. Thinking in extremes made it very difficult for April to access her resources.

Cognitive distortions of any type must be examined, analyzed, and challenged if we want our lives to be based on truth and sound, healthy thinking. How does one do that? It begins with looking for evidence. Is there any evidence to support the accuracy of this thought? Or, on the contrary, is there any evidence which disputes this thought? If so, how can I go about finding out the truth? Do I need to go on the Internet, to the library, read a book, consult an expert in order to discover what's really true? There are times when we don't want to challenge our thinking. As mentioned, cognitive distortions can be very protective. There are some things that we might prefer not to know or not to face. However, this is a barrier in creating a community of one. It encourages us to continue promoting the precedent that 'fudging' the truth to feel better for the moment is acceptable. This sort of logic typically backfires at some point. Creating a community of one is an exercise requiring great courage and as painful as it might be, only a foundation of truth and clear, accurate thinking will carry us through to that end.

Typically, part of the truth includes unpleasant emotions such as anger, fear, guilt, sorrow, grief, jealousy, envy, loneliness, or hatred. Strong connections exist between our thoughts and our feelings. Some have proposed that thoughts stimulate the development of certain emotions and others have proposed that it's emotions that bring about certain thoughts. If we're using distorted thinking to hide unpleasant thoughts, we may be doing ourselves a disservice. I believe there are some very positive purposes behind many of these uncomfortable emotions.

For example, anger typically occurs when we've experienced unfairness or injustice. A disruption in relationships has likely occurred as a result of the unfairness or injustice. Anger can motivate us to attempt to correct the unfairness or injustice and hopefully, repair the broken relationship. Grief over the loss of a loved one can be a precious feeling if we can remember it signifies the wonderful blessing of having been loved. Envy and jealousy make us aware that others have things that we lack. These feelings could motivate us to pursue our education or to go for the promotion or to learn some social skills. Hatred of evil in the world can push us into battle to help good to triumph. Guilt and fear are discussed in other chapters, but also have their positive sides.

Of course, all these emotions can be carried too far and can easily become detrimental. The negative aspects of these emotions can encourage distorted thinking and can effectively block all attempts of creating a community of one. Hatred, jealousy, and envy can very smoothly slide into prejudice, bitterness, and resentment. Sadness and grief can prolong into life-threatening depression. Guilt and fear can produce anxiety, worry, and paranoia. Not only do these negative aspects distort our thinking and block our creation of a community of one, they can make it impossible to connect effectively with a community of many. Vicious crimes are committed out of the negative aspects of emotions and distorted thinking. These vicious crimes include such horrors as Diana being battered to the point of death, Sue being denied the emotional support and nurturance of her parents, Maggie being sexually abused by her father and Uncle Ed, Maryanne being deserted by her unfaithful husband, or Dan being spiritually and emotionally abused by his church. Not all crimes are punishable by imprisonment but cause damage and destruction with far-reaching consequences just the same.

It is important not only to challenge distorted thinking to create our community of one, but it is also necessary to protect ourselves from the negative aspects of neglected distorted thoughts and the often comorbid or simultaneously occurring destructive emotions. Individuals who find themselves in need of creating a community of one are often in danger. Typically they are in precarious places in their lives and the future can go in one of two directions. This book is devoted to helping people understand their most difficult situations and helping them create a community of one. However, people can actively or passively choose to go a different direction. One could easily slip and fall into the areas of self-destruction or the destruction of others. Even for those who try to maintain the status quo, it is not possible. Change is inevitable.

Change can be positive and uplifting or it can be negative and destructive. Staying the same is not an option. The ground underneath a person will eventually erode and he or she is much more likely to slide downhill than up.

It is this tentative, dangerous place that will require a choice. No one is exempt although it is certainly harder for those who have had no training and who have little or no resources. Imagine trying to climb Mt. Everest with no equipment or extra food, or if you have those things, no knowledge of how to effectively use them. One can learn and one can acquire; but it is only through our choices to find knowledge and to work for resources. As much as we might like, no other human being can force us to make those choices. Few are freely given knowledge or resources with no effort required. Managing her lupus seemed like climbing Mt. Everest to Joan. As she encountered the storms of flares on her way up, she had to battle her thinking constantly: "the storms will never end, I'll never be warm or fed again, the storms are too great and I might as well give up." In struggling with her obesity, Laura likely thought the idea of climbing Mt. Everest was ludicrous. There were times when she could hardly get her body around the block, much less up a mountain. She would have to limit her food, her best friend and constant companion, trading it for warm, durable clothing that might not even fit in order to protect her from the elements. Where would she get the strength to climb a treacherous mountain, pit her body against strong, cold winds blowing down the mountain? The truth is that no storm in history has lasted forever. Even the great flood that Noah and his family endured only lasted forty days and nights.

Making the choice to create a community of one is the most difficult part of the journey. It is a choice that is made alone and in solitude. It is a choice that begins in our minds. Others will try to influence us or even try to tell us what to do, but they can't force the choice or the subsequent action required to make the choice a reality. This choice will require challenging the distorted thinking and destructive, negative emotions that might stand in our path. The choice will require emotional, physical, psychological, and spiritual work like we've never before imagined. It is a choice that will challenge us to dream of a vision, imagine goals, and believe in good things to come that we cannot now see. It is a choice that will force us to seek and face the truth of our lives, our situations, and our surroundings. It is a choice that can lead us to a place of peace and contentment no matter the situation. However, it is a choice made alone. It cannot be forced— not by family, friends, therapists, spiritual leaders, doctors—no one. The person in the mirror is the only ally in choosing to create a community of one or in choosing to move on to a community of many.

Chapter 13

Selecting Your Frame of Mind: Choosing Our Life Perspective

There is an old saying: you can see the jar half empty or half full. As simplistic as it sounds, it's very true. How we perceive our life circumstances can drastically alter our mental and physical status. Individuals who are interested in home decorating know this principle from experience. Presentation is everything in the creation of a particular perception. The same picture hung on the wall can project many different feels to the room depending on the frame used. A small, plain, black frame may project a very masculine, streamlined, modern look. The same picture set in a large, ornate, gilded frame may take on a more feminine, formal, elegant look. Yet the picture remains the same. Just as we can choose what type of frame we put around a favorite picture on our walls, we can choose the frame we put around our life circumstances. Will this change our circumstances? Of course not. However, seeing our life circumstances in a different "frame" may become a great encouragement to change those circumstances.

You may recall our story of Sue who struggled with alcoholism. Due to her drinking, she lost many things that had once been important parts of her life. The material possessions, the approval of her family, her successful career, her friends, and her status in society had all meant a lot to Sue. Her alcoholism stole these things from her in a very dramatic manner. Sue had a choice to make. She could feel defeated, depressed, a total failure, or she could see this situation as an opportunity to stop her current destructive behavior and set the course of her life in a new positive direction. Sue could resent the alcoholism as an interruption in her plan, as unmasking a facade she had worked hard to create, or she could see it as a positive challenge encouraging her to re-examine the values she held dear in life. Many see alcohol-

Becoming Your Own Emotional Support System
Published by The Haworth Press, Inc., 2007. All rights reserved.
doi:10.1300/5828_13

ism as a personal weakness. Others see it as a disease process. And there are those who might see alcoholism as a spiritual failure. Each of these perspectives might become a frame for how alcoholism is perceived. However, the frame does not change the fact that the picture of alcoholism is an addiction that brings about negative changes in the mind and body. Based on Sue's framework for understanding her alcoholism, she has several choices to make as to how she will respond to the problem. She might see it as a situation inspiring her to call upon greater internal strength. It might be perceived as a false friend or as a friend that will encourage a depth of character to emerge that Sue never before dreamed existed. Is this saying that alcoholism is a good and positive motivator? No, that would be ridiculous. However, it is saying that once negative events or a negative situation have occurred in our life, setting off things that cannot be undone, there are still ways to bring good out of these terrible, life-changing circumstances. They can often be redeemed.

Does changing frames change the picture? Of course not. However, the frame can determine if that picture is pleasing to look at. It can also determine if that picture fits in with the rest of the décor. Either the frame can enhance the appearance of the room, making it an inviting place in which to spend time, or it can detract from the room, creating a feeling of dissonance that is very unappealing and uncomfortable. April's wild behaviors that occurred during her periods of mania created dissonance with her otherwise interesting personality. When her illness was effectively treated or if she were in a remission, April's picture was that of a very intelligent, personable individual who was quite appealing to others. However, people were often very uncomfortable being around April during her manic episodes. The manic episodes put a frightening and macabre frame around her otherwise pleasing picture. According to E. Thomas Dowd and Terry Pace (Freeman et al., 1989), the power of reframing is found in the fact that once an individual has seen their situation in a different light, they cannot easily go back to their old perspective.

Some frames are cheaply made and reflect that, while others are very costly and greatly add to the value of the picture. A human picture is a work of art. Our character, our personality, our values, our goals, our faith, and so forth are not formed by happenchance. These attributes require work, effort, time to develop, a nurturing environment, and thoughtful care to become a picture of masterpiece proportions. The frames, or life circumstances, that surround our pictures will inevitably get banged up, gouged, nicked, or warped at one time or another. If we do not repair or change the frame, the picture inside will be in danger of reflecting that damage rather than reflecting the art which the frame was designed to highlight. We each choose how much effort we will put into keeping our frames in good repair and our pictures bright with color and texture.

To go back to the example of Sue: to value her sobriety more than her social appearance cost her a lot. She chose to no longer frame her life with a white Mercedes and expensive clothing. The frame she had been using for years was made of fake wood masquerading as expensive mahogany. However, the oak frame of sobriety that she now chose was very expensive in terms of relationships and her social standing. It didn't have all the intricate carvings that the mahogany frame did, in fact, it appeared much plainer, but in Sue's mind, the expensive replacement frame of solid oak sobriety completely changed her life for the better. Once she became aware that a frame of sobriety might fit her life very well, she was never again able to see herself in the frame of alcoholism. Even if she temporarily replaced the solid oak frame for the mahogany one, she would never be able to do so without remembering the satisfaction provided by the oak frame. There would always be a longing to return to the oak frame because it was so much more flattering to the picture of her life.

Laura needed to choose a new frame for herself. In Laura's situation, choosing a new frame for her life was very frightening. She didn't know what frame would most complement her personality and life goals. Laura had always reacted to the opinions of others, or at least what she assumed those opinions were. Her moods often reflected the disapproval she expected to receive from the people around her. This was like trying to hit a moving target, as the opinions of others change depending on the fads of the moment. Laura had never really trusted her own judgment in choosing her frame. She often bought into what the media said she should look like and then felt like a failure if she couldn't meet that standard. Laura never had the training or the resources to be confident in her ability to choose a complementary frame for herself. In creating her community of one, Laura had to choose her own frame regardless of what others thought. She might end up trying on many different frames before she decided which one would be most flattering to her.

Inexperience in choosing frames can lead to confusion and self-doubt. Similar to choosing a frame for a living room portrait, it is wise to try out several before deciding on the one that is the perfect match for our personality and life situation. Some frames are okay but bring no real life to the picture. They will do in a pinch and are better than nothing, but the vibrancy is missing. Diana had believed that she needed a dull, uninteresting frame in order to survive her abusive marriage. In her mind, a flattering frame would only bring more trouble on her head. As Diana began to create her community of one, she discovered that an attractive frame was initially frightening, and then, a pleasure. It had been years since she had come home to a life that was appealing and she grew to love it. When we're choosing a life frame we want it to be vibrant, the perfect complement to bring out all the important elements of the picture. We want a frame that won't highlight flaws, hide them, or pretend they're not there, but gracefully place them in the background. Just as certain colors bring out the best with our skin tones, certain life frames will cause others to say, Oh my!

The best life frames typically bring out positive character qualities. These qualities might include the courage to not give up, humility in facing our personal flaws, pride in our worth as a human being, kindness toward others when we have little to give materially, the integrity to do what is right even when that may take a fight, and so forth. When others see the picture of our life in this type of frame, it makes a positive impact that we may not expect. Others do notice our frames! Having our life attractively framed makes it much easier to transition from a community of one to a community of many. A dirty, scratched, dull frame will, in fact, cause others to avoid us. The possibilities of the picture will be overlooked. They will never know that a masterpiece lies hidden underneath the defective frame. Creating a community of one is like an artist restoring and bringing to life a work of art that has been hidden in an attic under a layer of dust and grime, unappreciated and unseen in its rightful place over the mantel.

It's not just how others react to our frame, but more important, it's how we react to the frame we've chosen. Dan's spiritual faith had been placed in a frame imposed upon him by the spiritual leaders with whom he had surrounded himself. He had completely submitted himself to their choices for what his frame should look like. Once Dan began trying out different frames, he began to get excited. Eventually, he chose a frame in which his faith was not dependent on the dictates of other spiritual leaders, but on his own personal relationship with God. This frame was pleasing for Dan to look at on a daily basis. He looked forward to getting up each morning and looking at the frame he'd chosen. Frames that others choose for us will most likely not be the best fit and we will not enjoy them nearly as much as when we choose the frame.

This was definitely true for Diana. She had allowed Matt to choose her frame and it was a terrible fit. On top of that, Matt's idea of the perfect frame for Diana often changed from day to day. She never knew what frame would be most pleasing. Matt's frame for Diana never highlighted her best features, it never drew out the possibilities of her picture, it never allowed the picture important focus. Matt's frame overpowered Diana's picture. His demands and his physical abuse caused Diana's picture to fade. If Diana had not chosen to create a community of one, her picture might have ceased to exist. Instead, she chose to change the frame to one that allowed her picture to have the spotlight and she began to touch up those faded colors. Over time, she became proud of her artwork and hung it in her foyer in a place of honor.

Choosing our frames takes time and careful consideration. It may require a lot of shopping around. The frame for our life should be a purchase that we spare no expense in acquiring. It will become an heirloom that will be passed on for generations to come. When subsequent generations look at our picture and its frame, what do we want them to see? Hopefully, we will want the richness of our frame and the quality of our picture to be an inspiration to others. It will be a guide, teaching others how to mix the colors, use the brushstrokes most effectively, and bring harmony and peace. It's not that we want others to copy our masterpiece, but we want our own picture to inspire others to do the same. Initially, however, our picture and frame need to help us create our community of one. There is nothing wrong with experiencing a sense of satisfaction with the framing of our lives. We can admit that we have talent, skills, and potential to create a masterpiece that will please ourselves and become a blessing to those around us.

Sometimes, the stresses we encounter may scratch even our carefully selected frame. It may have served us well for years. There's nothing wrong with refinishing a frame or touching up the scars to refresh the appearance so the frame continues to complement the picture to the best advantage. There are also times in which a frame may need to be replaced again. That's alright, too, as long as it's done with thoughtfulness and attention to healthy detail. Choosing a new frame can be one of the most fun and challenging aspects in creating a community of one.

SECTION III:
CREATING A COMMUNITY
OF ONE

Chapter 14

Sitting with Suffering:
Growing Through Grief

Sitting with suffering may be a challenging concept to grasp. No one wants suffering as a companion. Inevitably though, anyone who has needed to create a community of one has either already experienced suffering and has worked through it or, more likely, finds it is still hanging around. Trying to avoid suffering is denying oneself a solidly built community of one. Why is this? Because suffering has much to teach us that we can learn in no other way. Often, a short stint with suffering can lead to greater maturity and growth in character than years spent plodding along in relative peace and quiet. Henri Nouwen (2001) says, "Our efforts to disconnect ourselves from our own suffering end up disconnecting our suffering from God's suffering for us. The way out of our loss and hurt is in and through" (p. 7). What about going around, over, or under suffering? To go any other direction but through does not erase the existing suffering.

In and through what? What does it mean to suffer? Suffering will take on different forms for each of us. These forms are largely determined by the things we value, including relationships, financial security, faith, educational achievements, or physical health. The loss of something valued leads to pain, and that pain results in suffering. Pain is the constant companion of suffering. This pain gets our attention in significant ways. It can affect any part of our being—body, mind, emotions, and/or spirit. The amount and type of pain required to suffer is different for everyone. To cut one's finger while peeling an apple is painful, but typically does not lead to suffering as it heals quickly and is confined to a small area of our bodies. The pain of arthritis may mean constant suffering depending on how many joints are affected, how debilitating it becomes, and how long it has lin-

Becoming Your Own Emotional Support System
Published by The Haworth Press, Inc., 2007. All rights reserved.
doi:10.1300/5828_14

gered. Many would say that afflictions of the mind and spirit, though less obvious, cause more intense suffering than any physical pain.

The hardest aspect of suffering to grasp is that it is often purposely inflicted. We can inflict suffering upon ourselves or others can do the deed for us. This happens on all levels of human life. On a global level, it occurs as genocide, massacres, allowing mass starvation to satisfy greed, and the never-ending struggle for power that includes literally stomping people underfoot. The mass production of life-threatening illicit drugs that will destroy lives around the world seems endless. We hear about human slavery, using children for pornographic purposes, sex rings, and sex slaves. We see graphic images of people torturing other human beings and laughing as they shoot photographs for all to see. There are no words to adequately describe this kind of suffering. As a therapist, I have evaluated individuals from all over the world seeking asylum from unbelievable suffering inflicted upon them and their families by other human beings. Some of this suffering is so great that creating any kind of community of one seems beyond the realm of possibility.

On a smaller scale is the unspeakable suffering that is inflicted on people day to day, one person at a time. How could Matt beat Diana over and over again, lying and deceiving to explain away his actions? How could Uncle Ed and Maggie's father repeatedly use her for their own pleasure, ignoring the suffering they caused? How could Tom allow Maryanne to pour years of her life into his success and then willingly and purposely destroy her will to live, discarding her for another victim? There are no answers to these questions that will satisfy any sensitive person. But the situations are there and it would be dishonest to ignore them. Even though Matt, Uncle Ed, Maggie's father, and Tom may have experienced suffering of their own that distorted their thinking, that seems no logical explanation for continuing to perpetuate suffering on others. Logically, we would think that a history of suffering would lead one to be kinder to others, not ever more cruel. However, that is often not the case and there is no satisfactory explanation. In dealing with suffering there are no easy answers, just suggestions of how to deal with it in the most productive way possible.

Suffering often involves intense anger and rightfully so. Anger is a compelling emotion that is generated by injustice and unfairness. It demands that these wrongs be corrected. Yet there are situations where that is impossible. There is no way to bring back the innocence stolen by sexual abuse, no way to bring back a life taken by domestic violence, no way to indefinitely extend a life ravaged by an incurable disease. What do we do with this anger? There are no satisfactory formulas. We can harness the energy created by anger to do what we can to put things right. We can do whatever is within our power to mend the broken relationships resulting from the unfairness and injustice. Many times in the midst of our suffering, none of these efforts brings total satisfaction. So do we just give up? No. We acknowledge the anger as a good thing. There are many evils in the world and it would be wrong not to feel anger when we encounter them. Our anger motivates us to seek higher ideals, to work for the good of others as well as ourselves, and to call upon hope that the future can be better than the present. Our faith that God is in control of our world, even our suffering world, may be the one thing that gets us through.

The horrendous nature of suffering is often due to it separating us from people and things we enjoy, from the familiar surroundings we take for granted, and from our sense of safety. It may lead to fears about our future and what that future might hold for us. Certainly, suffering ensures that our future will never be what we expected or hoped for. Suffering requires us to see life differently, to learn new ways of dealing with things, and to relate to people in ways that may be very uncomfortable. Many people would describe suffering as the dark side of life, as an enemy. Henri Nouwen (2001) describes this well,

> Typically we see such hardship as an obstacle to what we think we should be—healthy, good-looking, free of discomfort. We consider suffering as annoying at best, meaningless at worst. We strive to get rid of our pains in whatever way we can. A part of us prefers the illusion that our losses are not real, that they come only as temporary interruptions. We thereby expend much energy in denial. (p. 8)

Unfortunately, denial never rids us of the suffering, at least not for any length of time. Are there any surefire ways to eliminate suffering from our lives? No, not completely. Even pain dealt with leaves a lingering aroma that can't be shaken. Parents who lose a child to Sudden Infant Death Syndrome (SIDS) may heal from their grief, have other children, and experience many joyful moments throughout their lives. They will never forget the pain of loss. Can anything be done? The only possible way to significantly decrease the amount of suffering in our lives is as Nouwen stated, to go in and through. Simply put, this means to accept and learn from the suffering. Can we realistically see suffering as producing a good outcome? Can we reframe this picture to make it something beautiful and appealing? There are individuals who have whom can give us hope.

One story that reflects that hope is the life of Tony Johnson (Johnson, 1993). He wrote a book about his life at age fourteen and if you ever desire to read a book on resilience and bringing good out of suffering, this is it. Tony's biological parents inflicted unspeakable suffering on him for years. They denied him the basic necessities of life such as a winter coat, a toothbrush, even a bed, and they beat him severely on a regular basis. They allowed others to use their son sexually. Tony and his friend, David, would often sleep on the New York subways because it was safer than being at home. At age eleven, in suicidal desperation, he called a national hotline in hopes of finding a reason to live. He did. A retired military officer and a social worker met each other through their efforts to help Tony, married, and adopted him. Tony finally had the family he had longed for all his life. Sadly, his suffering wasn't over. He was diagnosed with AIDS as a result of a sexual assault by one of his biological parents' friends. How did this fourteen-year-old boy deal with this unbelievable suffering? Listen to his own words,

> At the moment of my death, I want three things. I want not to be afraid. I want the people I love to know just how much I love them, and that a part of me will be inside them and make them smile every time they think about me. For someone who spent a great many years thinking that nothing good could come to me, I'm doing quite well. . . . Most important, I want to know that I have done everything that was humanly possible to contribute to my world in some kind of way. I want to give back in gratitude for having been able to be here. I hope that this story of a life well lived can be my contribution. (p. 211)

Unbelievably, Tony Johnson found the strength and courage to create a community of one amidst suffering few of us could imagine.

The lessons of suffering bring unbelievable strength to anyone creating a community of one. The first lesson is perseverance. Perseverance is the ability to stand firm no matter the situation. It is the ability to endure and even gain strength in the process of enduring. One may have had personal strength prior to the time of suffering, but persevering through suffering will deepen that inner strength in a way nothing else can. People often are amazed at the amount and depth of strength they develop through the course of suffering. With each new flare of her lupus, Joan recognized that she was more patient going through it. She knew better what to expect each time, and she knew the suffering itself would not kill her. This was not the case with the first few flares.

The second lesson of suffering revolves around the development of character. Character qualities most affected by suffering include patience, kindness, gentleness, self-discipline, courage, and honesty. Suffering individuals need to be patient as it may take more time to complete ordinary, everyday tasks. Individuals involved in a time of suffering may have to lean on others for help, perhaps requiring help for the first time in their lives. Suffering individuals may need to exercise kindness and gentleness toward themselves and others who might become impatient and intolerant. Sometimes the greatest part of suffering is the discovery that others may not be as caring as one had hoped or expected.

Self-discipline may be necessary to practice new skills or to learn to develop new, healthier habits. The natural human tendency is to gain everything needed in the easiest possible manner. Honesty and courage are also necessary. Suffering requires complete and total honesty to face the circumstances in which we find ourselves. Options must be considered from all angles and a path charted through the suffering. Honesty may require us to admit that things might not get better. The diabetic whose leg is amputated will never get it back. Irreconcilable differences in relationships may indeed be irreconcilable. Honesty may demand that we acknowledge that things will never be the same again and that some losses can never be recovered.

All of this demands supreme courage. Courage will be needed to sort through fears, doubts, and negative feelings. It will be necessary to help reach acceptance of things impossible to change. Courage will be needed to face obstacles external to ourselves, including friends and family who may not have our best interests at heart. Who would ever think that dealing with friends and family would demand courage? We hope for and expect love, support, encouragement, and approval from those whose roles dictate that we should be able to trust them to meet those needs. Courage may also be required as we face things about ourselves that we never wanted to recognize. Looking in the mirror and seeing missed opportunities, failures, unwise choices, and sheer foolishness is not a nice reflection. Courage will keep us on course through the suffering even if we must do it alone.

The outcome of suffering is peace. In a classic allegory Hannah Hurnard (1988) talks about the journey of a girl called Much-Afraid to the High Places. Along that journey, she encounters many dangers and obstacles, including her Fearing relatives who do not have her welfare at heart by any means. She often despairs for her life. Her companions on the journey are Sorrow and Suffering. Initially, Much-Afraid is fearful of them but has no choice in the matter of their companionship. As time goes by, she learns to lean on them and depends on them to teach her many things about herself that change her life. Once they reach the High Places, all three travelers receive new names. Much-Afraid becomes Grace and Glory, Sorrow becomes Joy, and Suffering becomes Peace. How can that be? We dread and fear what we do not understand. What Much-Afraid learned is that by shying away from suffering, we deny ourselves understanding and thereby the opportunity to grow.

Whether suffering is friend or foe depends entirely on how we treat it. Will we accept the lessons learned from suffering or will we fight against them to our dying breath? According to Henri Nouwen (2001), "Our choice, then, often revolves around not what has happened or will happen to us, but how we will relate to life's turns and circumstances. Put another way: Will I relate to my life resentfully or gratefully?" (p. 12). If we treat suffering as an enemy, it will drain us of all possible internal and external resources, and likely still result in our defeat. Although suffering may develop perseverance and endurance if we accept its teaching, suffering has a perseverance and endurance of its own to use against us if we don't accept. If we can accept the friendship of suffering, it will provide us with the wisdom and strength we need to take on any challenge in creating a community of one. This seems like an unbelievable paradox, but it is true.

Then there is this end result of peace. Once we have gone through suffering, we know that nothing can destroy the things that are most important in giving our lives meaning—our minds, our spirits, and our souls. Not only peace, but the freedom this knowledge gives is astounding. This is the sort of thing that causes the community of many to stand in awe of the person coming out of a community of one, a person who has persevered and developed character that's an example to all around. One prime example of this is watching disabled people participate in Special Olympics. Seeing the pride of accomplishment, the satisfaction of enduring through suffering to achieve often leaves the fans sitting in the stands in tears.

Learning to accept suffering gratefully can lift someone from despair and hopelessness, someone most certainly in need of creating a community of one, to a place of triumph. Nouwen (2001) states,

> Grateful people learn to celebrate even amid life's hard and harrowing memories because they know that pruning is no mere punishment, but preparation. When our gratitude for the past is only partial, our hope for the future can likewise never be full. (p. 19)

Imagine being in a place so low, so lonely, so seemingly hopeless that creating a community of one is your sole option to cope, and then to go through the suffering involved into peace and celebration. It is very possible and this can lead us to have hope in our suffering. Many would think that hope and suffering are completely incompatible and not to be spoken in the same breath, but that is not true.

To not have hope is to live life from a fatalistic perspective. This perspective suggests that no matter what we try, what we do, fate is against us and we might as well give up from the very beginning. People with a fatalistic perspective tend to be bitter, resentful, and cantankerous. They are not people who would in any way attract a community of many. In fact, a community of one would find them very unpleasant company. This is a completely different approach to suffering than discussed so far. It is not welcoming suffering with a grateful heart yet neither is it resisting suffering as an enemy. Seeing suffering as an enemy and mustering force to fight against it requires energy and action. There is engagement. To develop a fatalistic view of suffering is to do nothing—it is passively giving up.

If there is anything that is a hallmark of creating a community of one, it's not giving up! No manual on creating a community of one would ever have "giving up" in its vocabulary or index. Giving up is antithetical to the whole concept. It is deadly, more deadly than loneliness, suffering, or any difficult circumstance we might encounter. Unfortunately, giving up can masquerade as being realistic. One can say, "there's no way I can beat this cancer so why raise my hopes thinking I can overcome impossible odds? That's ridiculous!" Or, "I'm deformed, I'm in a wheelchair. Reality is that I live in a world that prizes beauty and stylishness. There is no way I would ever be allowed into a community of many, so why even attempt creating a community of one?" Individuals in these types of circumstances might lead themselves to believe that giving up is the only appropriate response to their suffering. This is deceitful and incredibly destructive thinking.

Don't fall into such a trap! There is much more to life than physical beauty and we do not have to be ruled by feelings. Feelings constantly change—maybe due to circumstances, maybe due to hormonal changes, or maybe due to the influence of others around us. To allow our feelings to be in charge is to consign ourselves to living an uncertain and unpredictable life. Living with feelings for a foundation is to live a life filled with insecurity. For example, many people feel that if they are unhappy in relationships the only solution is to break off that connection and begin a new relationship with someone else. They deny themselves the opportunity of growth in the relationship which comes by working through the unhappy feelings. The feeling of happiness comes and goes. It is very undependable. This feeds into the development and growth of fears, and fears, as we know, become a huge obstacle in the creation of a community of one.

Creating a community of one is more successfully built on solid evidence, evidence that supports the truth, obvious or not. This is a choice. Evidence typically doesn't come looking for us, we have to search for it. Sometimes we are afraid of the evidence we might discover but honesty compels us to discover it. Evidence may or may not support our feelings, but we examine evidence in spite of these feelings. Although I might not feel that I am attractive, if a number of unrelated people comment on attractive qualities I have, that would be fairly solid evidence that my own assumptions are not accurate. Maintaining a sense of low self-esteem based on my belief that I'm unattractive would be illogical based on the evidence.

Searching for evidence and honestly evaluating it will likely require courage. For April to face the evidence that she had bipolar illness, evidence such as racing thoughts, impulsive behavior, and severe mood swings, was a very painful process. This evidence also forced her to admit that the life goals she had previously set for herself would be unrealistic and unreachable. Her grandiose thinking fought hard with the evidence presented by her many treatment providers. However, in talking with others who also suffered from this mental illness, and in experiencing her own relief of symptoms when on medication, she came to the inevitable conclusion that the evidence overwhelmingly supported the prognosis given by her providers. Honesty led her to accept that evidence and consider what life changes she needed to make in order to create a community of one for herself. Of course, it is easy to accept evidence that supports our own position, but when the evidence directs us to unpleasant truths about ourselves or our circumstances, it is very hard to take.

Evidence can help explain suffering; it can redirect us away from suffering; it can help us endure suffering; but it can't make it go away. Creating a community of one requires that we acknowledge our suffering and allow its full weight to bear upon us. Then, and only then, can we use the weight of suffering to gradually build strength in our lives. No one ever goes to the gym and does a 300-pound bench press on the first day. The benefits that might be attained from suffering grow over time and then result in a cumulative effect. Those who have developed strength through dealing with suffering in their community of one will be able to make immeasurable contributions to a community of many. Does this mean we should seek out suffering so that we can ultimately make contributions to others? Absolutely not. It does mean that we should not shy away from the suffering that comes our way. Dealing with suffering constructively can be invaluable in creating our community of one.

Chapter 15

The Value of Vision: Creating a Map
for Future Direction

Imagine trying to get from Boston to San Francisco without a map. One could get stuck in a rotary in the Northeast and go in circles for days before figuring out the right exit. Who knows if you'd ever actually see the Golden Gate Bridge. Highly unlikely. That's what it's like to try and go through life without having a vision. You know you want to get somewhere and you know you want it to be a good place that you'll be happy in, but you may have no idea how to arrive there or what route to take. It is critical in life to have a vision, a dream. Particularly when a person is trying to create a community of one, he or she needs to have an idea of what he or she is trying to create. Initially, that's all it is, an idea. And a blurry one at that.

Typically, people who find themselves in need of a community of one have had a vision at some point in their lives. They may have had a vision of a wonderful intimate marriage and close family; they may have had a vision of growing into a strong faith that could never be shaken; they may have had a vision of climbing the ladder to career success; or they may have had a vision of living healthily into their eighties and beyond. Unfortunately, something happened and that vision was lost or changed. It became no longer viable for their current circumstances. Maybe the circumstances have changed to such an extent that the original vision can never be reclaimed. The loss of a vision may need to be grieved just like any other loss. We become invested in our visions and when they are gone or changed drastically, we feel lost and directionless and empty.

The loss of a vision can easily lead to a sense of hopelessness and depression. If I don't know where I'm going, why bother trying to get there? Without any guidance or direction, why should I spend my

Becoming Your Own Emotional Support System
Published by The Haworth Press, Inc., 2007. All rights reserved.
doi:10.1300/5828_15

limited energy just wandering in circles? And yet, it is in such times that we need to choose to create a new vision or revamp the old one. Again, that new vision may initially be only a glimmer of a thought. Nevertheless, we need to nourish and enrich that thought or idea until it becomes a beacon to lead us forward. Development of a vision will drive the creation of a community of one into the future. Don't get caught up in thinking about whether or not it's practical or realistic. In the beginning, just allow yourself to dream. For a four-year-old, it is developmentally appropriate to spend a lot of time in fantasyland. Four-year-olds pretending to be Luke Skywalker don't think about the impossibility of actually getting to the planet Hoth to engage in battle with Darth Vader. They just envision themselves becoming the best Jedi knight ever!

Practicalities can come later. The first step is simply allowing yourself to imagine that there is a new vision that can become yours in a special way. Then let that imagination go to the ends of the universe to discover what might be there. Once the door of possibilities is unlocked, you have something to work with and then gradually, you can think through the realities of claiming that particular vision as your own. Many people who find themselves in need of creating a community of one may not have entertained the notion of having a vision for years. They may feel they don't deserve a chance at having another vision. They may feel that creating a new vision for their lives is an impossibility because of the lack of resources or supports. They may be very fearful of trying again, of hoping again. However, I believe that *anyone* can have a vision for their life and can attain that vision.

The reason one needs to allow his or her mind to wander even into the realm of fantasies in creating a new vision is that the old vision may have been very powerful. It may have been so powerful and all encompassing that the only thing one can see for a long time is the smoke and debris of its crash. The old vision may have had very rigid boundaries, it may have been held together with strict rules that one would never dare to break or question, or it may have been imposed upon us by other very powerful people in our lives that we would not consider disappointing. In order to create a new vision, all those things must be let go or they will mire us down in depression and despair that could threaten to drag us under. It is risky, but we must allow ourselves to imagine the unimaginable.

Once we have at least an embryo of a vision, we can begin to think of goals that will lead us to actually living in the new vision. Goals must be realistic and attainable but also require genuine effort to reach. The basics of goal setting are establishing both short-term and long-term goals. Short-term goals need to be realistic and will determine the steps needed to reach those goals as well as our long-term goals; by building on the accomplishments of short-term goals we will reach long-term goals. Ultimately, we want to experience our vision for all it's worth! The absence of goals or goals that are meaningless leads to apathy and hopelessness. If goals are too easy, require little effort, and can be reached quickly, we take no pride in their accomplishment and we can develop a spirit of laziness. Just because we may have experienced devastating loss, or we may be up against seemingly insurmountable odds, doesn't mean our visions and our goals can't be challenging and admirable.

On the other hand, if goals are too hard, discouragement may make us want to give up and perhaps never try again. Our self-esteem can be damaged, and instead of developing an exciting vision with equally exciting goals, we may develop fear and avoid taking on any new challenges that might arise in the future. It's better to begin small and experience small successes than to try something that is genuinely out of reach in our current state. For April, successfully babysitting one night a week might be a realistic first step toward learning how to hold down a full-time job responsibly. It might be very fair to say that when changing directions and developing a new vision with which we have no previous experience, we may not know what is realistic and actually doable. If that's the case, start very small and try things out. Look for evidence at each step that will shed light on whether this is a goal to pursue.

These are some questions to ask in determining whether goals are realistic: Are there resources available to get started? If not, will they be attainable at a foreseeable time in the future? Are the goals within my range of talents and abilities? If not, do I have the intelligence and ability to learn new skills? Have I allowed myself a realistic time frame to test this goal and/or complete it? Don't be afraid to wholeheartedly answer these questions. As with many other aspects of creating a community of one, fear is the biggest barrier that keeps us from moving forward. Don't sacrifice your future or the enjoyment of a spectacular new vision because of fear. More will be said about that later, but all fears should be heartily challenged to see if they have any merit whatsoever.

Worry and anxiety are barriers that could possibly prevent us from reaching goals and seeing our vision become a reality. We rarely have problems letting our imaginations go wild when it comes to worry. We worry about what other people will think. We worry about making mistakes. We worry about failing. We worry about trying things that might leave us looking foolish in the eyes of others. We can literally worry ourselves to death. There is no question that worry can negatively affect our physical, mental, and spiritual health. An entire book could be filled with nothing but "what ifs."

There has been more and more research and investigation lately into the concept of resilience. Resilience is the ability to overcome difficult life circumstances and to move forward in a productive manner. It involves taking the risk to see our future going in a different direction than our past might have indicated. In their discussion on pursuing one's dreams and developing resilience, Brooks and Goldstein (2004) state

> there are no guarantees when we follow our dreams. However, it is far more effective to take action to change an unhappy situation than to remain unhappy and passive. When people take action, they are more likely to look for other solutions if the first one proves unsuccessful. Resilient people recognize that they can learn from actions that prove ineffective but they learn little, if anything, by adhering to an unhappy status quo. (p. 63)

Resilient people develop visions for their future and develop goals for how to get there.

Notice that most of our fears, worries, and anxieties occur when we become overly concerned about the responses of other people. Comparing ourselves to others can be deadly. Too often, we allow others to set the standards of what our visions should be. That can begin with parents saying, "Girls don't play in the dirt," to older siblings saying, "It's not cool to wear your hair in braids." If these statements are believed and if the approval of family members means more than anything, then some little girl will not think of envisioning a job in construction or of starting a new trend by wearing her hair in braids. Peer pressure takes great hold during adolescence. For a person to be popular and have friends hair must be worn a certain way, skirts must be a certain length, jewelry a certain type, and only a particular type of music is acceptable. Oftentimes, we may not even be aware of who set that rule in the first place. The young person who dares have a vision of his or her own may pay a very dear price.

Peer pressure doesn't just exist with adolescents. It follows us into adulthood and can hang around for years if we allow it. Advertising and marketing companies spend millions of dollars making sure we don't think too independently. It isn't profitable for them if people have individual visions. They are in the business of making us believe that *everyone* is eating at a certain restaurant, buying a certain brand of clothes, or watching a particular program on television. If someone is unwilling to conform, it is enforced with catty and sarcastic remarks, turned away faces, and few invitations to join socially with others. Don't think for a second that it doesn't take courage to develop a vision for your own life or that you may not have to fight to hang on to that vision.

When our eyes look with excessive concern toward others, we can't see the beautiful new vision that could lead us to create our community of one. To be overly concerned with what others will think or how they will react is a huge trap we must avoid at all costs. Others will not be around to experience the consequences of our choices. It is very interesting how America has been touted from the beginning as a land of opportunity, a country where each individual has the chance to be a success. That is still true in some cases, but more and more we seem to have become prisoners of the opinions of others.

Whether or not we can resist our fears and worries related to what others think will largely determine how successfully we reach our goals. We need to call on courage and commitment to our vision and goals in order to put aside our fears, worries, and anxieties and push forward into our community of one. Our vision and goals will eventually lead us forward into a community of many. The challenge at that point will be to hang onto our personal vision and not take on the vision of the community of many, whatever that might be.

Chapter 16

Tools of the Trade: Skill Development

For any new venture in life, we need new skills to achieve success. Developing a community of one is no exception. Once we have faced our fears, decided to take some risks, and developed some realistic expectations for our future, we're on our way. Approaching skill development as an exciting quest for adventure makes all the difference between experiencing it as drudgery or as racing for a prize. Typically, when a person finds himself or herself in a community of one, resources may be unknown, limited, or absent. Therefore, many of the skills described will cost little to nothing in terms of physical resources. They do involve time, perseverance, practice, and a willingness to try something new. Developing skills to become a community of one also equips people to graduate to a community of many with confidence and positive self-esteem.

The skills we develop, the steps we take, the self-care we do are not ends in themselves. They are only tools to help us with self-discovery. This is a critical point because many will find themselves still left with feelings of emptiness and disappointment if they follow the how-to plan and stop there. Creating a community of one first and foremost begins with knowing where we come from, who we are, and where we're going. We need meaning, purpose, and a plan. In his best selling book, *The Purpose Driven Life* (2002), Rick Warren talks about what often drives people in their daily lives. He suggests it could be guilt, resentment, anger, fear, materialism, or the need for approval. None of these driving forces will bring a person meaning, purpose, or a plan that matters. Warren suggests that purpose in one's life provides five great benefits: it gives meaning to life, it simplifies

Becoming Your Own Emotional Support System
Published by The Haworth Press, Inc., 2007. All rights reserved.
doi:10.1300/5828_16

life, it focuses one's life, it provides motivation, and it prepares one for eternity.

A word of caution is important as one embarks on this journey of self-discovery and the learning of new skills to create a community of one. This initially requires a focus on self, but in creating a community of one, we can't stop with self. To do so would be to forever stay stuck there and one would lose the ability to move on to a community of many. A very large part of our American culture is focused on "me"—*my* wants, *my* needs, *my* goals and so forth. An atmosphere of entitlement permeates every television commercial, magazine advertisement, and political agenda. If you stop to think about it, it's not even logical to think everyone can have their way all the time. The world doesn't have the resources to satisfy the exorbitant self-centeredness that we can easily develop. Clinically, this sense of entitlement is seen in personality disorders such as narcissism and antisocial personality disorder. What we're aiming for in creating a community of one is an *accurate* idea of self. An accurate perspective of self recognizes and owns our needs and desires but is also able to focus on the needs and desires of others.

As we can see, one can easily become completely self-absorbed in self-care. This will not be satisfying for anyone long term. Many times, individuals find themselves in need of a community of one because their lives have been out of balance. Maybe they have spent their lives in service to others at their own expense, ignoring personal needs and desires. This may very well result in disrespectful treatment by people who come to feel they can take advantage of another and never be called to account for it. Or individuals can become so focused on their own problems that they isolate themselves from any connection with others. They lose touch completely with the community of many, who may see them as merely selfish and avoid them as well. Neither excessive self-sacrifice nor self-centeredness will lead to creating a community of one and both will prevent one from healthily engaging in a community of many.

Balance is the goal. In creating a community of one, a person must realign his or her life to one of balance. This requires having an equally healthy and respectful appreciation for oneself and for others. It requires excellent self-care and excellent service to others. It requires recognizing one's limits and stopping before those limits are exceeded. It also requires establishing healthy boundaries with others and not allowing those boundaries to be crossed. It requires uninterrupted alone time for renewal and reflection as well as time for socializing and the enjoyment of others. As you read further in this chapter on skill building, please keep the need for balance uppermost in your mind.

Self-soothing. Have you ever noticed a baby who is upset over hunger pains that just won't go away? The baby's piercing screams and flailing arms and legs are a clear indication the world has come to an end from his or her perspective. Sometimes as adults we also feel helpless to get our needs met and it might benefit us to remember the kinds of things an infant finds soothing. Infants are primal sensory beings and it is through their five senses that they find relief. Although adults are also sensory beings, we often suppress those avenues of input in favor of cognitive functioning. Babies love to be covered in soft, flannel blankets wrapped tightly around their bodies. Imagine the comforting feeling of being wrapped in a long fleece robe, preferably right out of a warm dryer, and curling up on a soft couch in front of the fireplace. Most people would find it hard to move a muscle after getting in such a position.

Loneliness is often a cold feeling. Warm foods or drinks help us to feel warm inside. Afternoon tea has long been a tradition in some countries as a means to relax before finishing the day. Be careful not to overindulge in foods or drinks for comfort, but within a healthy diet choose foods that are soothing in terms of warmth and smell. Smells along with warmth have powerful, soothing qualities. Hot bread or cookies baking in the oven later combined with hot coffee or cocoa often give a sense of being cared for and comforted. We have to eat and drink anyway, so why not make selections that are healing to our spirit?

Our visual sense is also quite powerful in affecting our moods and motivation. Beautiful flowers in the spring remind us of renewal. If one can't afford to purchase flowers or doesn't have a yard in which to grow them, take a walk and pick wildflowers along the road. Flowers are not only a visual encouragement but also please us with fragrances. Many of the things which are most pleasing touch more than one sense at a time. Art is another medium which utilizes our visual senses and can fill us with pleasure, encouragement, and hope. Visiting an art museum can be an uplifting way to spend an afternoon, especially if followed by a fragrant cup of warm tea. Better yet, create your own art to reflect your feelings, thoughts, and spirit. Drawing, painting, and sculpting only scratch the service of possible art forms from which to choose. This is a powerful way of externalizing our internal world, especially for those who struggle with written and/or verbal communication. It often brings about a wonderful sense of release and freedom. It may even provide us with unique insights and understanding of things that mere thinking doesn't provide.

Self-soothing is such a critical skill because it comforts our hurts, eases our tragedies, and prepares us to take positive actions. If you find yourself in need of creating a community of one, there may not be others to provide soothing, as for example, when mothers provide for their infants. Self-soothing reminds us that we are worth being cared for, and that we are valuable human beings. It is easy to fall into the trap of believing that if no one wants to provide soothing for us, then we must not be worth receiving it. This is just not true! Self-soothing rejuvenates our spirits so that we are more capable of envisioning a future of better things.

Self-Discovery. It may seem odd to include self-discovery as a skill one needs to develop. But when people find themselves in the circumstances we have discussed, one of the most frequent losses is the sense of self, the knowledge of who we are outside of the terrible position in which we find ourselves. The abject loneliness we feel with great losses is partially due to the situation, but also may be due to the loss of who we believed ourselves to be. How do we discover the truth of who we are? That answer is necessary to begin the journey to developing ourselves as we want to be. There may be some things we discover that are unpleasant and distasteful; other discoveries may lead us to feelings of awe and excitement.

What were those hopes, talents, and dreams planted within the baby, child, adolescent, and adult before the defining event or circumstances that changed things forever? Too many times, we come to define who we are by events and circumstances and then carry that definition throughout our lives. For example, "I'm a diabetic," "I'm an alcoholic," "I'm a sexual abuse victim," or "I'm a divorcee." I argue that those definitions are not the soul of who we are. So who am I? It's time to find out.

Human beings are multifaceted in nature. Most people would agree that we are made up of physical, emotional, psychological, and spiritual components. Therefore, the skill of self-discovery needs to involve examination of all these components. Making an appointment with your physician for a physical examination is one place to start evaluating the physical angle. In preparation for that visit, write a list of questions you have regarding your current physical condition and what you might do to improve your physical status. It might also be worth at least one visit to a personal trainer to evaluate your physical status in terms of exercise, muscle tone, and stamina. Ask the trainer as part of that visit to outline a realistic plan for the time and financial resources you have available.

Our emotional and psychological components are often intertwined. Finding a quiet spot for meditation and reflection is a helpful beginning for examining these elements. Creating a safe, peaceful place in your home is an important starting place. It might only be a corner in a room, but that corner can become your refuge and oasis. Things to include in this oasis of space are: a favorite comfortable chair, good lighting, a favorite blanket and pillow, fragrant candles or flowers, the capacity to play soft, relaxing music, some encouraging and uplifting reading material, and a journal and pen for writing. Schedule regular time to spend in your oasis and establish clear boundaries with others so you won't be interrupted. This may be a more difficult exercise than you expect. If so, start with brief periods of time and increase them as you can. There is no set formula for what to think about or do during this time. One might start out by saying, "My name is Sue and I want to get to know and understand who I am." Don't be afraid to attend to the inner thoughts and feelings that will direct you to self-knowledge.

Some people may have experienced severe trauma and emotional disturbances in their past and even this seemingly innocuous experience of silent meditation might be overwhelming. If that is the case, professional assistance might be required to safely navigate this journey of self-discovery. Finances may be an obstacle to obtaining this service, but don't be afraid to ask for reduced or sliding scale rates. Many excellent therapists will oblige and work with you. If you live in an area where there are psychology or counseling training programs, you might be able to obtain free or low-cost therapy services at the training program clinics. Trainees are usually highly motivated to do well and are very closely supervised.

Finally, self-discovery involves examining our spiritual component. This aspect of our lives is often avoided because it may involve facing highly charged emotions or controversial beliefs. Shutting any difficult part of our lives in a closet and locking the door does not accomplish the goal of self-knowledge. So be brave and take off that dead bolt. How does one go about spiritual discovery? Many people have found that they have close ties to their spirituality in nature. Walks in the woods, on the beach, or through farmland, combined with a reflective spirit, can help in contemplating our creation and spiritual source. According to Rick Warren (2002), the ultimate goal of the universe is to show the glory of God.

> What is the glory of God? It is who God is. It is the essence of his nature, the weight of his importance, the radiance of his splendor, the demonstration of his power, and the atmosphere of his presence. God's glory is the expression of his goodness and all his other intrinsic, eternal qualities. Where is the glory of God? Just look around. *Everything* created by God reflects his glory in some way. . . . In nature we learn that God is powerful, that he enjoys variety, loves beauty, is organized, and is wise and creative. (p. 53)

There are hundreds of books written on spirituality. Reading what others have experienced, how others have traveled their own spiritual paths, and the struggles they've faced can help us examine ourselves and stimulate growth. Spiritual directors are available in many parts of the country and provide services free or at minimal cost. They are trained to help people explore their spirituality. A trusted spiritual leader might also provide such a service. Personal retreats are another common method to explore spirituality. Personal retreats are typically times when we find a more isolated place where we can befriend our "aloneness" and listen to our inner spiritual messages. Journaling and prayer are important parts of this exercise.

Books. A good book becomes like an old friend. We can read about the struggles of others and feel understood. We can read how they handled those situations and came through them intact. Sometimes the very problem we have causes us to feel so humiliated, embarrassed, and ashamed that we avoid others purposely. Those who struggle with addiction, like Sue, often feel like the scum of the earth and are terrified that they will be eternally rejected. Reading about people who have taken the risk of seeking and finding support they never dreamed was there can encourage someone to pick up the phone and begin to make connections. Sometimes we're stuck in our dilemmas because we just don't know what resources are available. Through reading, we can discover a treasury of places to go, people to contact, and interventions to try.

The wonderful thing about reading material is its availability. Libraries are free or charge only a minimal fee for an annual membership. Within the library of the twenty-first century are unbelievable resources such as audio books, journals, indexes, computers with Internet access, and of course, books in the thousands. Librarians are trained to help locate particular topics and don't require your personal life story to do so. You might come across a favorite that has been so helpful you decide to purchase it for future reference. There are now Internet services, such as Amazon.com, where used books in excellent condition are available for very low cost. Libraries are great places to "inspect the merchandize" before using limited resources to purchase. Many libraries and bookstores host book readings and signings by the authors. This is a great way to check out new material, get out of the house, have some free refreshments, and socialize (or not) without pressure.

Most communities publish free or low-cost local newspapers. These are great resources to see what's going on in your community. For people who are isolated by their circumstances and have lost or never developed a social network, local newspapers can inform them of events, services, support groups, availability of resources, and information about subjects of interest. It's a place to start reconnecting. Local access television stations also provide excellent information about interesting activities and events going on in nearby communities.

Music. Sometimes we just long to hear the encouraging voice of another human being. Sometimes other human beings aren't available and in our living room. Maybe everyone's at work and you're homesick and feeling miserable. Maybe you just moved to a new community and haven't gotten acquainted with anyone yet, certainly not on a deep level. You might be dealing with a dysfunctional family and you know it would be healthier for you not to go see them even though technically they're available. For whatever reason, that supportive, encouraging voice isn't present—at least not in bodily form.

Music is one of the most moving forms of expression. And it is available to the most poverty stricken individual. The great thing about music is that we have so much access—through the radio, libraries, and television concerts. Frequently, community groups and schools offer free concerts to the public. However, a word of caution is necessary. Not just any music will do. We have to be careful with our selections. Music has such a powerful effect on our moods that music with depressing, self-destructive lyrics can drag us down further, just as songs of hope and empathy can lift us up.

Music can also be a meaningful avenue of self-expression. If you don't know how to play an instrument, take up the challenge and learn. It can be expensive to purchase an instrument, but used instruments are available and that might be a reasonable choice. If you belong to a church, for example, you might even be able to make arrangements to play one of their pianos when rooms are not in use at no cost. Your voice is always free. You might not believe it to be the most finely tuned of instruments, but no one else has to know that! In playing or singing music for yourself, you can experience free expression from your very soul that is like nothing else.

Computers. Computers put unbelievable resources at our fingertips. In order to access these resources, it would be well worth the time to learn computer skills. Some groups offer courses for free or minimal cost to help individuals who are starting over. Courses to advance skills are also offered online. Community colleges, technical schools, and community adult education programs also offer courses. If a computer is unaffordable, libraries offer access for free. People can locate jobs, social connections, information, news reports, driving directions, and all sorts of things on the Internet. A word of caution is in order. One can deceive himself or herself into believing that he or she is being social and outgoing because of connections made over the Internet. This is an illusion. Some of these connections might also be dangerous. People can easily disguise their appearance, purposes, and agendas over the Internet. Use the computer for what it actually is, a resource to get started, not the end of the road.

Exercise. The word exercise may evoke many emotions for people. For those who engage in exercise regularly and feel the benefits, exercise is as necessary and natural as breathing. People who have never practiced the habit of exercise may see it as a burden on their time and energy that they can't afford. However, the benefits of exercise are hard to ignore. It increases our physical stamina and strength, decreases depression, increases self-esteem, improves our biological functioning, reduces the risk of disease, and enhances our appearance. Individuals who find themselves in a community of one will discover that exercise is a skill that anyone can develop, is accomplished in groups or alone, and is free to low cost. Of course, everyone should consult a physician before beginning an exercise program. Individuals with injuries or serious illness will especially need professional advice on the type and amount of exercise that might be helpful.

Once it has been determined that exercise is a safe and advantageous skill to learn, the fun begins. For people who might feel embarrassed about their skill level or appearance, videotapes or DVDs can be rented or checked out for free from the library. This is also a great way to try something out before making a purchase or investing in equipment. Another excellent way to begin gathering exercise equipment for use at home is to visit garage sales. Exercise is a tool we know is good and helpful for us in many ways, but it is a tool we often find an excuse to not use whenever possible.

Exercise may be an area of necessary risk-taking for many. For example, overcoming a fear of water to learn how to swim can lead to a positive sense of accomplishment, potentially expose one to another social set, and allow one to experience the soothing qualities of water. The novelty of learning something can be a motivator to maintain a higher level of interest, thus making the habit of exercise easier to develop.

The increased energy and sense of well-being that results from regular exercise will be invaluable for the person in a community of one who is trying to move forward in his or her life.

Volunteer Work. This might seem like an unusual suggestion in a chapter on skill development, but it actually serves many purposes. First of all, volunteering may actually involve learning skills that one could use in finding employment. It's a great way to get on-the-job training and also meet people in your field of interest who could connect you with paid employment. Second, volunteer work teaches us the skill of perspective-taking. When we are in the depths of despair, see no way out, and are prepared to just give up, we often start to drown within our own single-minded perspective. Helping others broadens our view of the world and may give us new insight into our situation. We might also be stimulated to try different approaches to improving our own lives.

There is no substitute for the self-satisfaction we experience when we know we've made a contribution to others who are also in need of help. This is one of the greatest antidotes to depression and despair and is definitely underutilized in the treatment of those problems. You may very well come across others who are in need of creating a community of one. Volunteer work may become a very natural transition from developing a strong community of one to becoming a productive member of a community of many. This is one activity where you can encourage others and also find encouragement for yourself. As mentioned, the one danger is becoming unbalanced. The very rewards you experience might easily suck you into giving more than you're able at this point in time.

We can use limitless tools in creating our community of one. These tools are the product of our imaginations and creativity. We can learn from others what has worked for them. It might not work for us, but a variation on a theme might be just what we need. Creating a community of one is just that—CREATING—with all the tools at hand.

Chapter 17

Never Give Up:
A Call for Hope

Hope. Neither a community of one nor a community of many can be built without hope. Henri Nouwen (2001) talks about hope being an expectation we have for the future. He says,

> The paradox of expectation is that those who believe in tomorrow can better live today; those who expect joy to come out of sadness can discover the beginnings of a new life amid the old; those who look forward to the returning Lord can discover him already in their midst. (p. 62)

No one can go through the intense pain of circumstances, the agony of facing their fears, the risks of learning new skills, or access the courage to move forward without hope. The hope I'm talking about is not wishful thinking, such as "I hope I'll get a raise in my next paycheck" or "I hope it works out for me to go to the Bahamas this summer" or "I hope I'll win the lottery" or "I hope that dress I want will still be on sale when I get to the mall." Even though those things might happen, and they could be motivating factors pushing someone to work some extra hours at his or her job, they are not a satisfactory driving force in one's life.

The key quality of hope is its future focus. Hope is believing that at some point in our future, our life will be better than it is now. It's seeing a giant, sturdy oak tree whenever you look at an acorn. It's seeing a man or woman of character working hard at being a doctor, a teacher, a mother or a father whenever you look at your two-year-old throwing a tantrum. It's noticing an empty bird's nest outside your window and seeing the beautiful red cardinals sitting on the trees in

Becoming Your Own Emotional Support System
Published by The Haworth Press, Inc., 2007. All rights reserved.
doi:10.1300/5828_17

the summer year after year. This doesn't necessarily mean that we will inherit great wealth, have servants, get our dream job, be free from physical pain, or find the perfect spouse. Hope that is based on these types of things will be disappointing and can lead to giving up. This is not to imply that none of this will happen. You might very well log onto eHarmony.com, an Internet dating service, and find your soul mate. Or through hard work and self-discipline, you might very well get your dream job. Wise investing could build a wealthy portfolio. But hope is not a guarantee that any of the things we think we want will come about.

This brings up the excellent question of what happens when the things I hope for most don't come about. What happens when after the first year of unemployment, there are still no jobs coming through and no interviews scheduled? What happens when the MRI comes back showing yet another hot spot of cancer on the lungs? What happens when I'm forty years old and I still can't seem to meet someone to spend my life with? What if my teenage son or daughter doesn't come home from a party on time and a police officer is ringing our doorbell at 4:00 am to tell us there's been an accident? Unfortunately, we know these situations happen all the time. We just hope that they won't happen to us. It may be a huge temptation to give up in despair and many people do. Circumstances are often so painful we just want to hide. Hope seems illusive or non-existent and all we can think about is escaping the pain. Drug companies make billions of dollars off prescription antidepressant and anti-anxiety medications. Alcohol and marijuana are also popular ways to numb emotional pains.

Then there are those things we believe we want most in life which turn out to be quite unsatisfying. Oftentimes, people who dream of having millions of dollars find that when they have it, the responsibilities and obligations that come with it make it difficult to enjoy. This brings up the question of whether or not we have the wisdom to know what is best for us. Many of the things we hope for provide us with only temporary pleasure and when that is over, we realize the consequences weren't worth it. Hoping for sexual excitement by having an illicit affair can easily end in disaster. Yes, initially it might feel like the thrill of a lifetime, everything you've hoped for, but the end results could be anything from contracting a sexually transmitted disease, to an unwanted pregnancy, to broken families, to losing a job, and to disillusionment when the excitement can't be sustained.

The possibility that we might not even have the wisdom to know what to hope for may seem like an absurd and silly notion. However, many of our hopes center around relief of current unpleasant circumstances. We want the pain to stop now, we want the loneliness to end now, we want the pressures of our jobs to end now, we want grief over the loss of a loved one to end now, we want our creditors to stop calling now. This is understandable. No one enjoys experiencing discomfort and pain for any length of time. While it is true that we may bring on discomfort and pain through poor and thoughtless choices, sometimes discomfort and pain come through no fault of our own. In either case, hope for immediate relief may not bring the peace and happiness we're looking for long term.

Remember that hope is future oriented. Even though it is not inherently wrong to hope for things in the immediate here and now, hope that will sustain us throughout our lives must have long-term implications. Again to quote Henri Nouwen (2001),

> This no to discouragement and self-despair comes in the context of a yes to life, a yes we say amid even fragile times lived in a world of impatience and violence. For even while we mourn, we do not forget how our life can ultimately join God's larger dance of life and hope. (p. 63)

The wisdom of knowing what to hope for comes with being able to see the big picture. The big picture includes not only this afternoon, tomorrow, next month, or next year, but also twenty years from now and into eternity. The great Biblical passage on love also includes a word about hope. "And now these three remain: faith, hope, and love" (I Corinthians 13:13, NIV). The implication here is that along with faith and love, hope will last forever, even into eternity. This is a very different kind of hope than "I hope I can lose twenty-five pounds this month" or "I hope I will get an engagement ring on Valentine's Day this year." Lasting, encouraging, peace-producing hope has a lifetime and eternity perspective.

What does this mean in practical terms for someone needing to create a community of one? It means hoping long-term, hoping with wisdom, and/or hoping for healthy change. This might mean a change in circumstances or it might mean a change in self. It's hoping that life will improve in some lasting, permanent way. Hoping in this way will require a shift of focus, a shift from considering only our current situation to considering implications for a lifetime and beyond. For example, for Maryanne, whose husband was unfaithful and abusive, the natural and immediate response might be to hope that Tom will have consequences for his actions and express genuine remorse for what he did to her. Maryanne might hope to skip the grieving and the work of emotional healing and just move on to being happy. She might hope that a knight in shining armor will appear on her doorstep and she'll have the marriage and family life she always dreamed of. While these are pleasing things to hope for, these are hopes that will not provide the long-term satisfaction that will carry her through life.

Wise hoping for Maryanne might include hoping that eventually Tom will experience remorse and learn to be a better person. This would likely be a long-term process. It's not easy to hope for good things to happen to someone who has deeply wounded us. In fact, it may seem impossible for a long time. Maryanne might hope to learn from her pain—Why was she so passive in the first place? Why did she not take steps to protect herself? Why did she place such little value on her personal worth? Why did she choose someone like Tom? Although this type of self-examination is painful and lonely, it will prepare Maryanne for a better future with healthier perspectives of herself and of relationships. The results of this type of hope will more likely reap the rewards of genuine satisfaction with a life that she really wants.

This brings up another point. Genuine hope is solid and unchanging. It is not dependent on fate, the whims of other people around us, or our own changing moods. It is based on dependable truths—eternal truths that will never change. Otherwise, our hoping would lead us on an out-of-control emotional rollercoaster ride. It is hard to hope for anything if the results of our hope are illusive, uncertain, and always changing. Dan recognized this as he was creating his own community of one. He had put his hope for support and encouragement in other people, namely his pastor and other leaders in the church. He had trusted them completely. He had trusted their integrity and their goodwill toward him. What he discovered was that their integrity and goodwill were conditional. Those conditions were dependent on their own desires and on how much Dan would be willing to contribute to them gaining those desires.

Does this mean that Dan should never trust anyone again, or that he should never hope for supportive, satisfying relationships within his church? Of course not. But people are always changeable to some extent or other. None of us are perfect and we will make mistakes. Dan discovered that his hope should not be in people, the best of whom will be imperfect at times, but in the God of his faith, who is never-changing and trustworthy at all times. With this shift in what he hoped for, Dan could then seek out healthier relationships in a church setting where other people are willing to grow and learn from their mistakes, people who shared his hope in an unchanging God rather than a hope that some other person will be everything they need. This is true for many people. They find that genuine hope is grounded in their spiritual faith and that that is the kind of hope that carries them through their earthly life into eternity.

Creating a community of one is all about learning to hope when there is no one to be supportive, not enough financial resources, and no physical energy to move forward. It is continuing to hope when dire circumstances seem unending and all those around you are tired of hearing about them, including yourself. When the messages you consistently hear are "you can't do that," "that's impossible," "you might as well just give up and accept things the way they are," you continue to hang on to hope. Not only hang on to hope, but learn to nourish it and watch it grow. This was the very litany that led Maryanne to need the creation of a community of one. Hope motivated her to see through the lies, the deceptions, and the distortions. Her hope initially was to see something better for her children. Somewhere along the way, she realized that the most hopeful thing she could give her children was a hopeful mother.

Creating a community of one means you have finally found yourself in a position where you may have to deal with the situation primarily alone. It can be a place of strength and it can be a place of rejoicing. That may sound strange but it's true. The hope that you can generate in a community of one is *your* hope, no one else's, and that can be a powerful place in which to be. It is a hope that will not change on someone else's whims or on the faddish thinking of society, or diminish when the one you have leaned on moves away. It is yours! Never give it up! This kind of hope goes beyond our failures and disappointments and helps us develop confidence in our own identity and worthiness as human beings.

Creating a community of one is only the beginning. No one is ever meant to permanently live in a community of one. It is a launching pad that will hopefully land one in a supportive, encouraging community of many. In creating a community of one, we come face-to-face with the hardships, struggles, disappointments, pain, and suffering that may have previously prevented us from satisfactory participation in a community of many. In coming to honest terms with ourselves, our Creator, and the realities of the life we find ourselves in, we gain strength and confidence to participate in a community of many with a newfound perspective.

Epilogue

A Final Word

This book could really be many books. There are many different stories told, many different situations highlighted, and many different suggestions for changing one's course. The examples highlighted in this book are only a few of the many scenarios that could possibly lead someone to need the creation of a community of one. Not even mentioned were situations of poverty, of physical disabilities—both genetic and acquired through accidents—and other chronic illnesses, both physical and mental. This book is one of real life. More people than we might like to admit find themselves in need of a community of one. Real-life situations provide evidence that there are many paths that lead to becoming a member of such a community. The danger for individuals and for society is that the community of one can become a bottleneck. People who become stuck in the community of one lose their sense of connectedness with the human race, and those who ignore their plight lose the joy of contributing to their own success.

The goal of successfully becoming a community of one is to develop a firm foundation from which to join a community of many. How does one know when one has actually created a community of one? This knowledge seems a necessary prerequisite to moving on to a community of many. A number of possible criteria come to mind when considering the creation of a successful community of one. First is adding being alone to our slate of friendships. This may seem paradoxical but it is the most solid foundational piece of the community of one. The enjoyment of being in one's own presence means not being so needy for the presence of others. It is the basis on which we can then freely make good and wise choices regarding the community of many we are considering joining. When we are at peace with our aloneness, it presupposes that we have cleared our conscience and

Becoming Your Own Emotional Support System
Published by The Haworth Press, Inc., 2007. All rights reserved.
doi:10.1300/5828_18

have developed a healthy degree of self-respect. We will have taken on that challenge to be agonizingly honest as we look in the mirror and will have come to like the image we see. We will have learned that truth is not something to be feared, but something to be embraced.

Second, in a community of one our achievements and possessions are no longer the focus of our existence. The approval and accolades of others is no longer the focus of our existence. Our focus is on our Creator, seeking His approval and following His direction for our life. This leads directly to the third criteria for a successful community of one—being at peace with ourselves and our purpose in life. There is a strong emphasis in our culture on having positive self-esteem. No argument here. However, self-esteem is often confused with self-centeredness. Self-centeredness seeks praise, approval, and encouragement no matter what the goals or behaviors might be. Genuine and positive self-esteem recognizes our strengths, our weaknesses, and our areas of mediocrity. All parts of the self are taken into consideration and either enjoyed, tolerated, or improved upon. Genuine self-esteem leads to being at peace with ourselves and it directs our purpose in life.

Finally, the number of friends we have is not the measure of social success in a community of one. Becoming our own best friend is the goal. Once that is accomplished, we will never truly be alone again. That is the jumping off place and at that point, we can branch out to develop friendships in a community of many. Those friendships can then be chosen and nurtured from a place of emotional, psychological, and spiritual health. There will no longer be a need to depend on people we may not trust, may not like, or may not admire. Friendships will become a choice.

As the author of this book, it is my ardent desire that those who find themselves in a community of one will be able to gain the strength to move out of their anguish toward peace and that those who are part of a community of many will reach out joyfully to include new members. What a satisfying experience it could be to have become a member of a community of one, joined a community of many, and then become a mentor to others struggling to form their own community of one.

References

Adams, C. J. (1994). *Woman-battering*. Minneapolis: Fortress Press.

Allender, D. (1990). *The wounded heart*. Colorado Springs, CO: Navpress.

Arterburn, S. & Felton, J. (1991). *Toxic faith: Understanding and overcoming religious addiction*. Nashville: Thomas Nelson Publishers.

Barker, K. (ed.). (1985). *The new international version study bible*. Grand Rapids, MI: Zondervan Bible Publishers.

Barkley, R. A. (2000). *Taking charge of ADHD*. New York: The Guilford Press.

Beck, A. T., Wright, F. D., Newman, C. F., & Liese, B. S. (1993). *Cognitive therapy of substance abuse*. New York: The Guilford Press.

Blume, E. S. (1990). *Secret survivors*. New York: John Wiley and Sons.

Bradshaw, J. (1988). *Healing the shame that binds you*. Deerfield Beach, FL: Health Communications, Inc.

Brooks, R. & Goldstein, S. (2004). *The power of resilience*. Chicago, New York, San Francisco: Contemporary Books.

Brownell, K. S. & Fairburn, C. G. (eds.). (1995). *Eating disorders and obesity*. New York, London: The Guilford Press.

Courtois, C. A. (1988). *Healing the incest wound*. New York, London: W.W. Norton & Company.

Doka, K. J. & Davidson, J. (eds.). (1997). *Living with grief: When illness is prolonged*. Bristol, PA: Taylor & Francis.

Engel, B. (1990). *The emotionally abused woman: Overcoming destructive patterns and reclaiming yourself*. New York: Fawcett Books.

Enroth, R. M. (1992). *Churches that Abuse*. Grand Rapids, MI: Zondervan Publishing House.

Freeman, A., Simon, K. M., Beutler, L. E., & Arkowitz, H. (eds.). (1989). *Comprehensive handbook of cognitive therapy*. New York: Plenum Press.

Geller, B. & DelBello, M. P. (eds.). (2003). *Bipolar disorder in childhood and early adolescence*. New York, London: The Guilford Press.

Hurnard, H. (1988). *Hinds' feet on high places*. Wheaton, IL: Tyndale House Publishers, Inc.

Johnson, A. G. (1993). *A rock and a hard place*. New York: Crown Publishers, Inc.

Johnson, B. C. (1996). *Good guilt, bad guilt: And what to do with each*. Downers Grove, IL: InterVarsity Press.

Johnson, D. & VanVonderen, J. (1991). *The subtle power of spiritual abuse*. Minneapolis, MN: Bethany House Publishers.

Becoming Your Own Emotional Support System
Published by The Haworth Press, Inc., 2007. All rights reserved.
doi:10.1300/5828_19

Johnson, J. (1993). *When food is your best friend and worst enemy.* San Francisco: HarperCollins Publishers.

Linn, S. (2004). *Consuming kids.* New York, London: The New Press.

Manning, B. (2000). *The ragamuffin gospel.* Sisters, OR: Multnomah Publishers.

Manning, B. (2003). *A glimpse of Jesus.* San Francisco: HarperCollins Publishers.

Manning, B. (2005). *The importance of being foolish.* San Francisco: HarperSanFranciso.

May, G. G. (1988). *Addiction and grace.* San Francisco: Harper & Row, Publishers.

McFarland, B. & Baker-Baumann, T. (1990). *Shame and body image: Culture and the compulsive eater.* Deerfield Beach, FL: Health Communications, Inc.

Miller, M. S. (1995). *No visible wounds: Identifying nonphysical abuse of women by their men.* New York: Fawcett Columbine.

Nadeau, K. G. (ed). (1995). *A comprehensive guide to attention deficit disorder in adults.* New York: Brunner/Mazel Publishers.

Nouwen, H. (2001). *Turn my mourning into dancing: Finding hope in hard times.* Nashville, TN: W Publishing Group.

Pollin, I. (1995). *Medical crisis counseling: Short-term therapy for long-term illness.* New York, London: W.W. Norton & Company.

Roberts, A. R. & Roberts, B. S. (2005). *Ending intimate abuse: Practical guidance and survival strategies.* New York: Oxford University Press, Inc.

U.S. Department of Health and Human Services. (2006). *"Weight-control information network."* Bethesda, MD.

VanVonderen, J. (1989). *Tired of trying to measure up.* Minneapolis, MN: Bethany House Publishers.

Walker, L. E. A. (1994). *Abused women and survivor therapy.* Washington, DC: American Psychological Association.

Wallace, D. J. (1995). *The Lupus Book: A guide for patients and their families.* New York, Oxford: Oxford University Press.

Warren, R. (2002). *The purpose driven life.* Grand Rapids, MI: Zondervan.

Index

Becoming Your Own Emotional Support System
Published by The Haworth Press, Inc., 2007. All rights reserved.
doi:10.1300/5828_20

For Product Safety Concerns and Information please contact our EU representative GPSR@taylorandfrancis.com Taylor & Francis Verlag GmbH, Kaufingerstraße 24, 80331 München, Germany

Batch number: 08158885

Printed by Printforce, the Netherlands